PRAISE FOR DEBRA MONROE

"Fine and funky, marbled with warmth and romantic
confusion, but not a hint of sentimentality."

—*Boston Globe*

"Rangy, thoughtful, ambitious, and
widely, wildly knowledgeable."

—*Washington Post*

"Her characters, like her prose, have hard edges. They also have
big hearts, dark humor, and purely unique ways of opening
themselves up for our inspection. This book makes you want to
take the author out for a drink and tell her your troubles."

—ANTONYA NELSON

"If this book were a country song,
Lucinda Williams would sing it."

—*Atlanta Journal-Constitution*

"Prose that shimmers like a jazz solo."

—JONIS AGEE

"Her intelligence tilts the world and offers her every encounter
an almost hysterical spin. In a [book] laden with trenchant notes
on our new world, Debra Monroe offers us a lively quest—
a woman caught between the romantic and the semantic
evaluates all the fangled possibilities for human connection."

—RON CARLSON

"Intelligent . . . deliciously wacky."

—*Publishers Weekly*

My
Unsentimental
Education

John Griswold, series editor

Also by Debra Monroe

My
Unsentimental
Education

Debra

Monroe

The University of Georgia Press
Athens & London

© 2015 by the University of Georgia Press
Athens, Georgia 30602
www.ugapress.org
All rights reserved
Designed by Kaelin Chappell Broaddus
Set in by 11/14 Filosofia Regular
Printed and bound by Thomson-Shore, Inc.
The paper in this book meets the guidelines for
permanence and durability of the Committee on
Production Guidelines for Book Longevity of the
Council on Library Resources.

Most University of Georgia Press titles are
available from popular e-book vendors.

Printed in the United States of America
19 18 17 16 15 C 5 4 3 2 1

Library of Congress Cataloging-in-Publication Data
Monroe, Debra.
My unsentimental education / Debra Monroe.
pages cm
ISBN 978-0-8203-4874-2 (hardcover : alkaline paper) —
ISBN 978-0-8203-4873-5 (ebook)
1. Monroe, Debra. 2. Authors, American—20th century—Biography.
3. Women authors, American—20th century—Biography. 4. Working class
women—United States—Biography. 5. Single mothers—United States—
Biography. 6. Monroe, Debra—Relations with men. 7. Man-woman
relationships—United States. 8. Sex role—United States. 9. Working class
families—Wisconsin—Spooner. 10. Spooner (Wis.)—Biography. I. Title.
PS3563.O5273Z46 2015
813'.54—dc23
[B]
2015005541

British Library Cataloging-in-Publication Data available

I am aging and eaten and have
done my share of eating too.

—ANNIE DILLARD

CONTENTS

My
Unsentimental
Education

Near the turn of the century, the recent turn, fragrant jasmine wafted and crowds of students milled. I sat on a bench near a bronzed statue of a young Lyndon B. Johnson carrying textbooks, his necktie flapping rigid as he strides toward his future. He's the university's most famous graduate, also known to have said, perhaps apocryphally: "If it wasn't for public education I'd still be looking at the ass end of a mule." If it weren't for public education, I thought, I'd be a small-town waitress, divorced with grown children by now, haughty with boredom. But I was forty-something, a professor with a baby daughter, and Miranda, a student I was about to teach, sat down next to me and told me that the new day, the new season, springtime, inspired her. Apropos of not much else, she said, "I'm glad to have such a modern role model. And I always admire your shoes too." I glanced at her sideways.

I didn't feel like a modern role model.

The faces of previous students—Jennifer, Alyssa, Melissa, Kim, Samantha, Anne, Whitney—reeled past. They'd initiated parallel conversations. In my office, with books and papers stacked askew. Or, if spring had arrived, outside, like this—sap rising, dull roots stirring (lilacs, desire), students passing in pairs. In one version, the conversation implied I'd made an appealing life blueprint and followed through. In another version, I'd sacrificed womanly longing for Great Literature. Neither account is true, Gentle Reader. But I never said so. Pretending life has progressed according to plan is part of anyone's job. And once, when I was just two years older than a student named Lucy—I still remember her anxious, square-jawed face, how she'd sublimated all her worries into a master's thesis about Victorian heroines too bluestocking to marry—I'd even pretended at home.

Lucy's parents didn't trust her judgment, she'd explained, so they'd asked to meet me. I wasn't the first woman in what used to be a mostly male profession; I was part of that first mass wave of women entering it. Some of us used to correct our well-meaning elder colleagues who called us *my dear* and praised our hairdos, not our work. I didn't, though, having clocked in for years at jobs where correcting your superior got you fired.

Lucy's parents stopped by my house, which Lucy's mother reflexively praised—a rental house filled with eccentric used furniture. Lucy's father shook my hand. "Ah then," he said, "you've answered my question already. You're wearing a wedding ring." I nodded. At the time, I was at the tail-end of a grim starter marriage: my second. My husband would have been at work. Or so he'd say. Sometimes he was. Planning how to extricate myself, how to divorce with the least fallout, was currently taking up more mental room than the book I needed to write to keep my brand-new good job. But I didn't volunteer that to Lucy's parents. Publish or perish, I thought, pouring iced tea into tall glasses.

You publish and die anyway, hopefully later.

"Married and a lady professor too," Lucy's father said, smiling.

I smiled back. This was just one version of myself: temporary.

I'd already been so many.

I moved away and got divorced. And now Miranda, who'd grown up ten years later than Lucy, ten more years of seeing women in white-collar jobs, sat beside me. Her aunt had a career, she said. "And she always has an exciting new boyfriend too," she added.

This aunt must live in a city, I thought. Or this was the public account of her private life. Or I was projecting. I wanted a man who'd match my old self, my new self, all my selves.

So far I'd met Either and Or.

Either. The night before, I'd gotten back into bed with a moody jack-of-many-trades I'd dated erratically for years—breakups, makeups, seeing him lately after dark as my daughter slept in another room, the baby monitor on my nightstand blinking green, serene, a can't-last-much-longer arrangement, true. But I couldn't change where I lived, half-rural, half-highbrow. The night before he'd said he felt objectified. He hadn't even known what the word meant when I'd met him, but he heard one of my friends say it and asked me to explain. I had, citing the standard complaint about *Playboy*—not that it's sexually candid, but that its depictions of women don't seem real. Maybe objectification is a woman-to-man problem, I thought. Because my first impulse had been to tell him that we would discuss feelings later, but go ahead and objectify me quickly because the baby might wake, and I had to get up early, my Monday morning to-do list long. But I didn't. I lay there, silent. He got dressed and drove away, his headlights angling into the dark.

"Where does your aunt live?" I asked Miranda.

"San Francisco," she said.

Or, for example. Before I was a mother, I'd ignored the impracticality, the costly phone bills, and I had a boyfriend I'd met at a professional conference. We visited each other when we could. Mostly we gave good letter. I know the appeal of a sentence bent to please its reader, a glimmer of emotion solidifying to a point. I sent my own letters back.

The fact that he loved me astonished him, he wrote once. Prone to genteel locutions, he said my letters arriving in his mail slot caused his heart to quicken. My heart acted odd too, but I thought it was jitters. He lived in a faraway city. He had a girlfriend already. Instinctively monogamous if a bit hit-and-run, I wasn't good at being the Other Woman. I'd been raised with stark ideas about purpose: a woman who surrenders all to others, good; a woman who wants (covets), bad. Though I'd been taught to think more subtly since, first impressions last. Yet I hadn't let go because he was the only man I'd wanted to sleep with who could discuss John Donne, the history of the English language, Aristotle, *The Selected Poems of Federico García Lorca*. Our brains matched. Our bodies did. Remorse mixed with desire. The letters amassed. My heart thudded.

Once, in an especially well-crafted paragraph, he said he'd dreamed a man in bib overalls stood next to me on the other side of a river, urging him to stop stalling already and cross over. Annoyed, I'd wondered: Why is a farmer my matchmaker in this dream? Because I kept a tidy house and sewed well? Because a hound dog slept on my porch? Because I'd lived in provincial towns and cities all over? My long-distance lover took the dream-advice seriously. In a real city, he moved out of the upscale home he owned with his girlfriend.

I started planning what to do and say.

His letters arrived two and three per day now: a tumble of script an imprecise substitute for a man, I noticed. Then they stopped. I felt scared. Tricked. I broke out in hives as I graded papers and listened to records. *Someone to watch over me.* Whether or not you have this, whether you feel lonely as the clock creeps toward midnight, is a personal problem, I decided. Work is necessity. Love is for evenings and weekends. He called ten days later. He'd never found a moment during one of our trysts, or during one of his letters either, to tell me he was epileptic. He'd had a grand mal seizure due to the stress of contemplating a new life, and the seizure was real, he said, not the cockamamie dream.

Before either of these men, there'd been more. Scads.

One night a friend from graduate school had called, worried her number was too high.

"Number?" I'd asked.

"Sex number," she said.

"People count that now?" I said. "Isn't it also how many people you've loved?"

"Loved?" she said.

"Until you change your mind," I'd added, confused. "Until it doesn't pan out."

Sitting next to Miranda, I felt the urge toward truth this time. Because the world churns out aphorisms about school days, golden rule days, school the investment that always pays. But for me—improbably educated yet addicted early to books, convinced that what I'd read and remember would be honey in the larder for tedious years ahead—school had been a time of growing into one life and then another, another, changing social backdrops, lovers, husbands, each time hoping my new life would be the last revision. Men I'd gone to school with had heard women were their equals. I'd heard this too. But it was recent news then. We'd all been raised in homes where women weren't. I usually dated down anyway, because dating up was work. Work was work, pretending to be who I wasn't yet, pretending to be self-assured and expert by day. So at night and on weekends, I'd wanted to stop pretending. I chose men as if I'd never left home.

Tamping down a too-personal inflection in my voice, I told Miranda I couldn't imagine myself without my job—my "vocation," I said, using my work-day dialect. But, I said, I understood that having pursued it meant I'd bypassed turn-offs to other lives. Scraps of antiquated prose were free-floating around my brain. *The angel in the house*. *Facilitating the family dialectic*. I said this out loud: "I wanted to be the angel in the house."

Miranda frowned. "Angel? Is that a New Age idea?"

"No," I said. "It's an old idea." I explained that Harriet Beecher Stowe, who wrote for magazines and newspapers, not just the little novel that started the big war, had argued that a wife and mother did civilization's essential moral work. I'd read Harriet Beecher Stowe in a class where the professor had emphasized that this accommodationist argument had helped set back women's rights. I secretly admired it. I knew its logic by heart. It was a flattering way to describe the only options I'd once had. But times change. I'd changed, improvising. I'd made my piecemeal life, ragged stiches between phases.

Miranda said, "But anyone can be a wife and mother."

I turned to Miranda suddenly. "Look, it was all a Plan B, C, and D." I described my job interview here, two days of campus meetings with committees, the dean, the provost, the president, a last appointment with the hiring committee chair, who'd described the job's details, a chair who was a woman, rare enough then. She'd said, "I confess I'm envious of you young women coming straight through with your PhDs. I waited for my husband to finish his degree, next for my children to go to school. Then I got my degree and put together a career as best as I could." Disarmed by this unvarnished moment during three days of official posing and hand shaking, by the distinct flicker of regret—she was in the midst of a divorce, I'd heard—I blurted, "Are you kidding me? I had dozens of failed relationships. At a certain point, I realized it would inconvenience no one if I got a PhD."

The hiring committee chair had glanced away, embarrassed.

Miranda was smiling. "So your career happened instead?"

"Yes," I said, "by accident."

History and
Practical Math

On my mother's side, my grandmother was a teacher, the undisputed sovereign of a one-room school. Then she married a man she met at the fair. At their fiftieth wedding anniversary party—when I was twenty and thought I knew everything, or more than my over-the-hill relatives celebrating days of yore, not progress—I saw a photo of my grandfather, wearing spats, pants too wide to be respectable, standing next to a roadster, and nearby a woman who isn't my grandmother wears one of those fur coats with dead animal heads dangling, and she sits on a road sign shaped like an arrow, her rump covering its letters. My uncle, who'd assembled the slide show, had included this photo. I glanced at him. Defiant, he was staking a claim for men's right to roam. Or he was still mad at his father.

I studied the photo, the vamp draped over the arrow. "Who is she?" I asked. One aunt giggled. My mother said, "Shush." My grandfather threw back his head and laughed. My grandmother—her hair lavish, intricate, shellacked as a crown—looked aloof, this long-ago affront irrelevant because of fifty years of prodigious regeneration, children, grandchildren, great-grandchildren. My grandfather used to leave every fall to sell the harvest, I knew. He was supposed to return with cash and shoes for the children. But, having gambled, he'd return with no money, just someone's silverware or, once, a Shetland pony he'd packed into the Chevy's backseat. My mother had told me that my grandmother, gardening, canning, cooking, sewing for six children, would sigh and go inside.

After the slide show, everyone left for spare bedrooms in scattered farmhouses belonging to relatives. My mother and her siblings were tipsy, so I drove. One aunt asked my mother why my dad hadn't come. My mother didn't answer. My aunt said, "Why didn't he?" My mother let go: "Because he couldn't make the effort. Are you happy?"

My mother and father had argued.

She hadn't told her siblings because everyone bowed down before the finality of marriage, and she thought my dad would too, in time. Marriage suffers insult, then self-repairs.

My aunt said, "You should have set aside squabbles for one day." We were at a stop sign, and my mother flung open the door and ran in heels and a DuPont faux-silk dress into moonlit fields. I stopped the car and ran after her. Sobbing, she fell into my arms.

I'd assumed that only young people have sex and therefore only young people feel tragically rejected. Yet here was my mother, tragically rejected. My heart hardened. I didn't want to be her. I didn't want to be my grandmother, who'd married a man who wasn't her equal in terms of ambition because ambition had added up to zilch without a man.

Both of my grandmothers lived in North Dakota. The other was famous for her cooking—homemade sausage, kuchen, calf's liver in sour cream—but also for having schizophrenia, though no one called it that yet. She gave birth to her first son in a sod house, and later to my father and another son in a wood house. She ran away when she got the chance, rebelling.

Or crazy. Strangers brought her home. Someone used to lock someone else in the corncrib—an airy, aromatic prison, I used to think, with its weathered, silvery slats and golden litter of corn. Either the sons got locked up when my grandmother didn't feel well, or my grandfather locked her up until the cows got milked, the hay baled. She might hit a son with a skillet, or she'd stop cooking, and the sons would have to walk to town in a blizzard to charge food at the general store. My mother, sister, brother, and I doubted a few of these facts. Some of them must be true. But my dad exaggerated, we knew. All those years without good mother love had made him need extra attention now.

The grandmother who'd been a teacher, then a mother, then a teacher again—a modern teacher in a brick school in town—had been a taskmaster too long. She might have tried to be impartial at school: uniformly cranky. But as a grandmother, she had grandchild-pets and grandchild-dunces. Some of us got to decline the grassy-tasting milk we called cow milk and she tried passing off as store milk by sneaking it into a carton she'd borrowed from someone. The rest of us choked it down. One cousin invented words while playing Scrabble and got praise. I invented words and got barred from the game.

Yet you couldn't tell she liked some grandchildren better than others from her Christmas presents, seventeen versions of the same item. One year it was a scrapbook, *My School Years*, Kindergarten on page 1, First Grade on page 2, all the way to Twelfth Grade. You filled in the blanks: My Grades; My Favorite Subject; My Hobbies and Activities. Each section ended with a checklist, "What I Want to Be When I Grow Up."

The "What I Want to Be When I Grow Up" checklist, with separate categories for Boys and Girls, listed Mother as the first Girls' option, followed by Nurse, Teacher, Secretary, Stewardess. Boys' options didn't list Father at all, just Doctor, Banker, Fireman, Policeman, Farmer, Pilot. This discrepancy bothered my sense of symmetry, an aesthetic sense, not a desire for parity. I hadn't noticed parity yet, or not as it applied to girls.

I liked the infinity of possible futures at the end of this checklist, a blank labeled Other. One year I wrote "missionary." Church no doubt contributed to this vision of myself evangelizing while wearing white. School would be a story, I realized, leading me toward The End. An escalator lifting me. I'd enter the fray, irregular, but finish with a smooth life that would be rewarded in people's thoughts and conversation, the best shot we have at immortality, the praise or gossip that outlasts us. Yet during my real page 1, Kindergarten, I understood that school, if not the scrapbook about it, required hard-core bluffing.

I tried out facial expressions. My teacher, named Mrs. Gagner, taped children's mouths shut. I haven't invented this name. I've remembered it these years because, at the time, I thought all words would shimmer into meaning if I paid attention. Mrs. Gagner had either always been her name or turned into it. She used Scotch tape first. If it didn't stick, she upgraded to masking tape. She didn't tape everyone's mouths shut, just whisperers'. One day at nap time I lay on my rug with Scotch tape on my mouth, hoping I seemed stoic. A girl on the rug next to me—a girl I barely knew because she was Catholic and her father owned a bar—lifted the hem of her skirt to show me that, since her dress didn't have pockets, she was carrying her new box of Crayola crayons in her underpants.

When First Grade started, I wasn't there. We lived in Spooner, Wisconsin, where my dad sold auto parts. Besides brutal stretches of winter, when subzero temperatures turn engine parts brittle, summer was his big season due to tourists' broken-down cars, so he had to work to make money until after Labor Day, and then we rushed to a hospital in North Dakota where my grandfather, the one married to the wandering grandmother, lay dying.

We children stayed with the taskmaster and the gambler. While my mother and father familiarized themselves with the sick grandfather's care and made plans for the wandering grandmother's future, the taskmaster grandmother lost track of my little brother, who crawled into a suitcase and ate aspirin. My parents came in from the hospital, turned around and went back, my mother holding my brother. His skin was transparent, veins like blue rivers. Doctors pumped his stomach and yelled at my mother, she said.

When we got home, kids in my First Grade class were looking at letters in clumps and, in a thick-tongued way like Helen Keller, saying these letters as words, clump after clump accumulating into sentences about Dick, Jane, Spot. I was called on to read a word: "see." Instead of sounding it out—no one had taught me to spit, glide, or vibrate consonants and moan vowels, let alone spit and moan sequentially—I recited letters. "S," I said, "E, and E." Then we were freed to recess on a playground where louts of boys and tall girls holding hands as they chanted "Paul, Ringo, George, and John" ran circles around me. I recognized a timid boy from my class in a red sweater with kittens on the pockets. We walked hand in hand, which made big kids circle nearer, faces swollen with menace.

The teacher phoned my mother, asking to keep me after school. The teacher explained phonetics. The code broke. I could read "See Dick run," also the *Superior Evening Telegram*. And books from the library, or bookmobile, or shelves at home. My mother had bought the complete Dr. Seuss, the *Encyclopedia Britannica*, a series called *Folk Tales from around the World*, and every month the mailman brought a volume of remedial adult novels, *Reader's Digest Condensed Books*. Obsessed with the lives of made-up people, I pondered stories—why this character did that, new outcomes, possible sequels.

I ignored the teacher, lessons, the dandruff-flecked neck of the boy in front of me. Reading, more exciting than life, calmed me. I was as high-strung as my wandering grandmother.

My wandering grandmother lived with us now, and my mother worried aloud that I'd inherited her tendencies. Waylaid by Reading, I didn't concentrate on Math, Geography, Science. And behavioral aberrations were considered outages of willpower. I never witnessed one of my grandmother's spells. She was rushed out of the room and usually spoke a mix of English and German. But she saw dead people and described events that might happen as if they already had. She slept in my brother's room on a bed called the rollaway and came to breakfast in a nightgown with a hairnet over her curlers, her mouth collapsed (either the sadness or missing dentures), and belched and farted. She was a big, homely baby.

I reached out to her by giving my doll a German name, Gisele, and asking my grandmother to swaddle her, because this grandmother was good at swaddling. When I left for school, I said Gisele would need to eat, and I handed my grandmother a toy bottle of fake milk that drained when you tipped the bottle—like novelty ballpoint pens my dad got from traveling salesmen that, right-side-up, showed an ordinary cartoon woman but, upside-down, showed her ink-clothing draining away, her naked orb-buttocks and cone-breasts.

One day my grandmother ran across town without a coat, and if the mailman hadn't called us we might not have found her before she froze. She'd chased him, she said, because she'd written to a man who'd advertised for a German-speaking wife, and she wanted an answer. Of course, we didn't believe this. And my doll had lain unfed because my grandmother couldn't pretend, or that's how she left babies after swaddling them.

Meanwhile, I was falling behind in every subject except Reading. I'd daydream, thinking about, let's say, Rapunzel's mother, who craved rampion, not unlike spinach, the dictionary said, and in the days of thatched roofs people believed that not satisfying a pregnant woman's craving caused deformed babies, so it was right to steal the rampion. Yet the father traded it for the unborn baby, which canceled out my idea that this stealing was justified, not greedy. These people—characters, mere words on a page—had maybe never existed. But their thorny landscape, their sketchy moral bargain, their fears and expediency, kept me from focusing on multiplication or the Ice Age. Or on dusting and vacuuming.

At home, it was just five of us again.

We'd moved my grandmother back to North Dakota, to a hospital where doctors first said she was schizophrenic. We thought she'd split into two, but, no. Her thinking was fragmented. We didn't belabor the diagnosis because our family doctor didn't understand it, and the encyclopedia was confusing: daguerreotypes of the man who'd named the disease, lists of symptoms (insomnia! olfactory hallucinations!), descriptions of patients who thought their brains had been invaded by TV. My grandmother started taking first-generation psychotropic drugs and married the widower who'd advertised for a wife—my parents first met him in her hospital room when he arrived with a box of chocolates.

When we visited her, we ate all day, playing cards and sipping beer, shot glasses of beer for the children. At night my sister and I crept down the basement steps, past the iron jaw of the sausage maker, past pipes and a hellish furnace, to a plywood guestroom with a bed and a dresser covered with plastic flowers and dozens of framed photos of the widower's dead wives, dead but still alive in the photos. Someone had moved the photos and graveyard flowers down here. The first wife was God-fearing. So were her children. The second wife's children grew up and went to prison.

At home, my mother had hung a plaque on the wall. CHARACTER IS WHAT YOU REALLY ARE. REPUTATION IS WHAT YOUR NEIGHBORS THINK YOU ARE. You might guess this meant she worked at character and scoffed at reputation. No. The plaque consoled her that even if she didn't have a reputation, good or bad, just invisibility, she had character. Turning into shopkeepers in a small town with exacting gradations, my mother and father said that we didn't care how we seemed. But we did. Dinner conversations—this man had ten children but worked hard and bought a new car; that man had a fun personality but no grit—ascertained people's rank, which was malleable. My parents measured people's attitude and fortitude, which you control. They'd staked their futures on the belief they could.

Middle school was called junior high, and the building, 1960s-era, containing grades Fifth through Eighth, sat next to the old-fashioned high school with Doric columns and sequestered offices at the top of curved stairwells. I'd pass through the corridor that connected the schools, carrying a note from a teacher in junior high to someone in a lofty office. School was cold, but this corridor was hot, an engineering mistake. I spent my lunch hour there, next to an auditorium with a stage that had a mechanical folding wall the janitor cranked open for dances involving a king, queen, and court. It was shut most of the time and covered by velvet curtains with weights in the hem. I rolled myself against the collapsible wall, letting the curtains wrap around me. Then I'd unroll and do it again, swathes of velvet like vestments, and once I bumped into someone coming from the other way who turned out to be a boy, and we rolled apart again, afraid.

What else?

A red-nosed teacher said I drove him to drink. "It's not a figure of speech," he added. I stared at his wild hair and bloodshot eyes. I lacked the ability to fail then prevail. I didn't always do homework and tried to save face by answering in diction from another era. "We were put on this earth to persevere, you as well as I, sir." Or, caught reading a novel in History: "There is no frigate like a book to take us lands away." I didn't try to make adults unhappy, and yet—I wasn't the first adolescent to notice this—adults made so many decisions and I made few. One day in spring, false spring because we usually had a last snow in May, a breeze blew through an open window. I climbed out. The teacher yelled. My hair snagged on a bush. Dead grass was turning pale green at its roots.

I got sent to the principal. My mother, bookkeeping at my dad's store, showed up, angry. Then she ran out of steam. She seemed to know that my best wasn't like anyone else's.

In the summer, we lived in our cottage that once belonged to people who'd died. We'd acquired their Oriental rugs, their horsehair love-seat, lamps with hand-painted globes, antique vases. The cabin sat on a lake carved by glaciers—shallow plateaus in the center but, here and there, inches from shore, drop-offs so deep no one had fathomed them. My parents, sister, and brother went to town every day, my sister to her summer job, my brother to stock shelves at the store. I stayed behind to cook. That left hours for taking the boat across choppy waves. I'd slow to enter a creek connecting our lake to another, where I'd cut off the motor to hear wind whistling through trees, bird ruckus, the shout of a human reverberating bell-like over water. I studied houses. A piney woods effect here. A paradise effect over there, patios with striped umbrellas out of place next to a barn.

One afternoon, lying on the boathouse roof, reading *Love Story* by Erich Segal, I felt hot enough to think it was summer, not summer's imitation. Truck drivers delivering beer to taverns honked as they passed. So far honking meant "I know you" or "I'm trying not to run you over." Uneasy, I went inside. I had a pet rabbit. We hadn't bought him a cage, so he'd grown tame, housebroken, hopping everywhere I went, whimpering if I left him. He crouched on the bed as I looked in the mirror and saw that, if I squinted, my swimsuit made me look like someone else. In a few years I'd be making my selection, I understood, a local man, and I'd better get ready. Then I unsquinted and looked like me again, a girl. We moved back to town in the fall. The rabbit stayed in a neighbor's cage with other rabbits. In a week, he'd gone wild, back to rabbits, and wouldn't let me hold him.

I dove deep into the fracas of high school—including kids who lived in town, also kids who rode the bus and smelled like barn—where my sister was a cheerleader and Rodeo Royalty (doubling as "Miss Spooner and Her Attendants"). She followed rules. On weekends, she drank and made out because these were rules. So was not getting caught. I objected to not-getting-caught. Over the summer I'd read *The Autobiography of Malcolm X*; *My Darling, My Hamburger*; *A Tree Grows in Brooklyn*; *One Flew over the Cuckoo's Nest*; *The Catcher in the Rye*; *Mr. and Mrs. Bo Jo Jones*. The national zeitgeist, disestablishmentarianism, had trickled down by way of the paperback book rack at Rexall Drug.

I'd get grounded. Then sprung. Then grounded. My parents didn't object to jocks, but I knew them as mean, then friendly after dark, trying to take my clothes off. Stoners were called heads. "He has faraway eyes," my mother said about a head whose mother had died. "He has a sickly sweet odor like a spice rack," she said about another. She was paraphrasing the Warning Signs Your Child Might Be on Drugs. I didn't smoke pot, but I didn't mind if people did. I made out with heads, practicing my kissing. Like my sister and my parents, I knocked back alcohol. Drinking erased anxiety and social distinctions. My dad drank with people who were fun but didn't have grit. Heads and jocks drank together in hunting camps with bunkrooms: squeaky bedsprings, whispered moans.

Then I met a man at the fair.

He was short with a grown-up's head and shoulders. If he'd been taller, he'd have been uninterested in a fourteen-year-old waiting to ride the Rock-O-Planes. He worked for the phone company, repairing connections in the office, in people's houses, on top of tall poles I noticed with a sense of awe for his daring vocation as I rode down highways in my mother's car. He lived on his parents' farm because his dad had a bad heart. By now, my sister was pre-engaged, a friendship ring with a diamond chip. This thrilled my taskmaster grandmother, who'd been single and considered a spinster until she was in her twenties. My wandering grandmother was young—the census record is sketchy—when she married. I'll call my elfin, muscled boyfriend Rodney V. Meadow, a synonym for his real name. V is for verdant. Life teemed with allegory.

On Saturday, I'd go to dinner with Rodney V. Meadow, who bought buy-one-get-one-free coupons to supper clubs—restaurants deep in the woods. People arrived by snowmobile or in cars with tires wrapped in chains. After dinner, we made out in his truck.

I wondered: Were sperm airborne? What did "vigorous swimming" mean?

I fell ill, wondering. My mother, who bought sanitary napkins in bulk, said, "You're moody because your period is late." One night in my bedroom, my alarm clock ticked on. I gave up on biology and focused on plot—foreshadowing and upshot. In our living room, with its imitation brass lamps aglow, Pledge-polished furniture gleaming, my mother's face would crumple. It had crumpled a few weeks earlier when one of my classmates got out of a car at school wearing a maternity dress hemmed as a mini. My dad would pour brandy with one hand, hold his other over his heart, as he did when he told you he was hurt (often) or grateful (rarely). I'd cook for Rodney V. Meadow when he came in from the phone company, I realized. After my baby became a child, I'd serve cupcakes at the elementary school. In a few years, I'd be like my mother, only younger, with modish dresses and silver eye shadow. Outside, dawn crept over snow-covered houses. I crept to the phone in the basement to call Rodney and tell him we were getting married.

The walking downstairs must have released muscles. I was instantly not-pregnant.

When I talked to him that weekend, he explained I couldn't have been pregnant because we hadn't had sex. He knew because he and his dad sometimes hired a bull and watched it work. He'd had sex himself, in the past. He'd like to again, he added. I couldn't trust myself not to, I knew, and I didn't want to squander another series of days and nights worrying how I'd feel moving to a stout house with hodgepodge furniture, or wheeling my baby through SuperValu as I bought meat, eggs, Comet, Gerber products, Windex.

In 1974, in Massachusetts and Wisconsin, The Pill was newly legal for single women. I'd read this in *Time* magazine. The decision about minors was pending. I forged a "please excuse Debbie from school" note, walked to a phone booth, and called every doctor in the Greater Spooner Area. Receptionists would tell me the doctor was with a patient, so I'd say: "Would he prescribe the pill to a seventeen-year-old without parental consent?" Most hung up. One said, "You should pray." Anonymous, I dialed on. Then a receptionist said, "Honey, Dr. X won't, but if you call Dr. Y in Shell Lake, he will." I forged another note, and Rodney took the afternoon off work to drive me to Shell Lake.

Rodney would wait in the truck, we decided, one less person to get noticed by an adult we might know. I'd never been to a doctor without my mother before. The receptionist checked off my name and went back to reading *Good Housekeeping*. I worried how to act. The only other patients in the waiting room were an elderly man and woman, attending to their old age or dying, which had nothing to do with me and never would, I thought, coldhearted, wrong. I pretended to myself that I was a wife. The Pill was new. Abortion, which we'd discussed in Social Studies because of *Roe v. Wade*, was new. Buck up, I told myself.

Yet what if someone walked in and knew by my face that I'd decided on a bad life: premeditated sex? What if the woman on the phone had set me up and the doctor would tell my parents? Still, I had to postpone getting pregnant, I thought, willing myself calm. For how long? *Que sera sera*, Doris Day sang.

The future is never ours to see. The receptionist called my name. I met Dr. Y. He told me to disrobe and left. I wasn't quite undressed when the nurse came back and complimented my modern, lace-knit bra, like this was gym class, the locker room. "So comfortable," she said, this woman old enough to be my aunt. Then Dr. Y came back and narrowed his eyes. I was in the stirrups, draped with a fusty hospital gown. I wasn't embarrassed for this part, or I'd known it was coming and I was ready. I shut my eyes. The doctor probed. He asked my age. I was fifteen. I said I was seventeen. Silence. He seemed not to believe me, but he gave me a year's supply of pills, which Rodney stored in his tool locker.

Soon, my parents let me spend weekends in the Meadows' spare bedroom because my mother felt farm chores were salutary. Or she was glad I'd stopped dating heads. She'd made local inquiries. People who knew the Meadows family attested, approved. The whole town weighed in, it seemed. This would be a good match in due time.

One day, I drove the tractor while everyone loaded hay. Rodney's father clutched his chest and turned purple when, after he'd expressed doubt I was the right person to drive a tractor, I took a corner too sharp. The tractor started tipping, one side of the hay wagon climbing a big wheel spinning in midair. Rodney sprinted across the field, leapt to the top of the tractor, reversed it. The tractor righted itself. The hay wagon rolled back down, its axle and my life saved. That night, Rodney's mother told me that no one starts out as an expert. We watched *The Carol Burnett Show*, and she taught me to embroider pillow slips and dish towels. When I saw my wandering grandmother, who embroidered, I showed her my work. She said my knots on the backside were messy. A backside should be as good as a front. I tried harder and piled up pillow slips and dish towels, though, as my mother noted, they'd look ragged after one time through the spin cycle.

In theory, halcyon summer was June and July. But intermittent cold fronts blew in, shrinking our allotment. I loved wandering through swampy patches of wildflowers, or rows of midsummer corn like a dense, miniature forest. My dad bought my brother a motorized mini-bike I'd borrow to ride through pine trees until I found abandoned houses I'd explore for signs of life—a tattered curtain flying like a white surrender flag in a cracked window, a rusty kettle on a stove. Once I saw a bear on a back porch, and I scrambled back to the minibike and sped off, my wheels stuck then swaggering through sand.

One night Rodney and I sat staring at cattails in a shallow lake, the radio tuned to a top-forty station hundreds of miles away. For a moment, John Denver's song about his ex-wife seemed like poetry—reasonable poetry for a man who hunted and fished, I thought, eyeing Rodney. *Night in the forest. Mountains in springtime.* Rodney could discuss these. Maybe they filled up his senses. But he couldn't take the next step and equate bliss in the woods with bliss he felt spending time with me. Could I live the rest of my life never hearing words like these said to me? I couldn't. But a day later, ironing my father's shirts, I turned sensible. Poetry was extravagance, I decided. Everyone has longings.

During short, dark days of winter, Rodney must have had his longings because he'd go to a bar after work and come to pick me up late, drunk. It would take me ages to forgive this, though my sister's boyfriend did it too, and my dad missed every second or third dinner the same way, and my gambling grandfather used to leave my taskmaster grandmother for weeks. Once, my mother stared at me, sitting cross-legged on the console stereo, a coffin-shaped box with a turntable inside, as I stared out the window, waiting for Rodney's truck. She said: "That's marriage. It's never our turn." She felt bad for me, but it wouldn't do any good to object, she said. The world was designed for husbands. She forgave my dad his lapses because wives did. He'd had that sorry childhood too. There's no use bemoaning the past, she said. But she said it to us, not him.

Then a teacher who wore narrow ties, not because they were in style, but because he'd never bought the new, wide ones, explained that impartiality is an ideal existing outside the toils of language. "A selection of facts is partial," he added, "partial as in incomplete, partial as in biased." He said I should go to a summer camp with students from all over the state, students between their junior and senior years, at a small college in Eau Claire, eighty miles south. For two weeks, I'd stay in a dorm and take writing classes. I did the math. I was a misfit at Spooner High. I'd be a misfit times fifty. I said no.

He rolled his eyes and didn't bring it up again.

Months later, false spring again, and I was walking to my after-school job, stepping through slush, wearing a pastel dress with my winter coat flapping open. A southern breeze stirred branches flecked with buds doomed to freeze before they'd sprout again. Anomie, acedia—sins I'd studied in Lutheran catechism, two hours on Tuesday night. My desire exceeded my portion again. I couldn't face belabored spring, fickle summer, flashy autumn, immense winter, seasons moving and standing still. I fastened onto a word I'd read but didn't know how to pronounce. *Ennui.* Suddenly I started running, twisting my ankles in my sandals with plastic fruits on the straps. I arrived at work early and phoned the school. The teacher was already gone. I tried his house, no answer. His wife ran the register at Rexall Drug, so I went across the street and told her I wanted to go to writers camp, and I jotted this down, and she said don't bother, she'd tell him.

That July, when I arrived at writers camp, my fears returned.

Then I faked that I felt at ease, and I did.

Some of the writers looked like heads. Some looked like cheerleaders and jocks. The cheerleaderish girls whispered that two girls looked like sluts, but I could tell the slutty-looking girls were just shy, from the same small town, and painted each other's eyeliner on too thick. I was nice to the eyeliner girls, to the cheerleader girls, and to a girl who looked like Carole King and quoted the *Tao Te Ching*. I also made friends with a boy named Michael who signed his essays and poems Mikal. My Favorite Subject was every class. My Hobbies and Activities were reading the assignments and staying up late to discuss them. As days flicked by, a boy from Fond du Lac stared across crowded rooms. His name was Chuck. He was my age but five inches taller than Rodney, I noted, disloyal.

I'd read Chuck's poems in class. They weren't interesting, but I felt that Chuck—dark and brooding—might be. We hadn't talked yet because Mikal stopped me after class, standing in front of me, his arm on the wall, challenging my opinions, combative flirting.

An alternate future opened up. Either Chuck or Mikal, I realized.

Mikal talked all the time. Chuck was silent. If the strong, silent lover found in books caused me to believe in a strong, silent lover sitting near me in a classroom, or if the fantasy of the strong, silent lover sitting near women everywhere causes his double to recur in art, is a chicken-or-egg question. Yet women fill silence well. They customize it. "Every night I give my body to my husband like a chalice," a woman wrote in a letter to Ann Landers I'd read in the newspaper, my interest piqued. As long as Chuck didn't talk, he was a void into which I poured thoughts so profound he apparently found them inexpressible.

The night before the last day, Chuck and I sat on a bench, hands touching. You shouldn't have sex before marriage, I knew, but I'd long ago arrived at this variance: it was okay if you did with the man you'd marry because you'd die having had sex with just him. So I'd reasoned until Chuck from Fond du Lac wanted to kiss me. I stopped him as Jane Eyre stopped her wedding. Except I'm candid. Some people appreciate this. Some don't. And you never know which kind of person you're talking to until after you've divulged. Instead of saying I was practically betrothed, hence unavailable, I said I wasn't a virgin.

He didn't speak. I'd planned to marry soon, I added.

I considered telling him I was on The Pill, because I wanted him to understand my life—that I'd been caught in the local pattern and I found the safest way forward, but if I'd lived somewhere else I'd be someone else and still could. Then he'd tell me he'd never met anyone so stalwart, so perfect, and we'd reunite at college in eighteen months. But he looked afraid and hurried off into the gloaming and avoided eye contact the next day.

That night, my parents arrived to take me home. They'd been confused by the whole episode, that I'd wanted to go, that I'd won a prize. They were used to prizes for best jam, best sales record for radial tires in the tristate area, best football playing—not best use of figurative language. We drove under interstate overpasses that seemed like cattle gates, one after another hanging over me as I passed through the chute toward home.

Rodney V. Meadow took me to supper clubs I used to like, to the farmhouse where I'd helped his mother make casseroles. I couldn't focus. I had trouble kissing him. He lost his temper and called me Miss Poem. One evening he was waiting for me to come downstairs for our date. It was early fall because my family, minus my sister, who'd gotten married, had moved back to town. My mother sat with Rodney on the side porch covered by trellises that made the room seem mysterious and stately. But my parents wanted a modern house, so they'd installed orange indoor-outdoor carpet and bought avocado green slipcovers for the furniture. When I got downstairs, I could tell my mother was in deep conversation with Rodney. She said, "We would have liked for you to marry her. But you gamble when you date someone so young. She's a girl, still deciding."

That night, after dinner, he drove back to my house and parked in the driveway. I told Rodney I wanted to go to college and we should break up now, as I began Twelfth Grade. He started crying. He put his hands around my neck. I thought his message was that he could choke me if he wanted but he loved me so he wouldn't. He'd lettered in wrestling—he had a wrestler's compact body, slow patience too. My mother paced back and forth in the kitchen window. As I spoke, muscles in my neck moved against Rodney's grip. I said, "I can't help it. I'm sorry." His hands tightened. He still didn't seem violent, just out of options. He let go, then put me in a new hold, my head banging the dashboard as I rolled onto the floor. He landed on me. My mother had begun flicking the porch light on, off. Then she stood in the driveway, rapping on the truck window.

One night, after snow fell, he waited in the truck while I went inside to get the framed high school graduation photo his mother had once kept on the TV but let me take home to put on my nightstand, and the class ring that had thrilled me with its size and unfamiliar date—I'd been in Eighth Grade when he graduated. I opened the door and gave them to him. He threw them into the snow. My mother called me inside. I watched from the kitchen. She stood in the driveway in her bathrobe, shivering, talking to him. He slumped behind the steering wheel. Under the halo of the porch light, my mother dug in snow and found the picture, which she gave him. She looked for his ring but didn't find it until the next day—guessing where it was by marks in the snow—and we mailed it to him.

He called from work, plugging a receiver into a random outlet. He also called from bars, music clanging and drunken shouts as backdrop. He called from the barn, cattle lowing. He called from the tops of telephone poles. He'd done this once or twice in the past when he'd be working late, thirty feet off the ground, a leather harness wrapped around his hips, boot cleats dug in deep, and say something cheerful, sweet. But he phoned now to say, for instance, he was on County Trunk 71, south of Mueller Road, and go mute, waiting for me to volunteer that the last weeks had been a mistake. After a few minutes of silence, I'd say I had to go. He'd call back. My mother started intercepting calls. I'd hear her, gentle at first, eventually firm: "You need to accept facts and climb down that pole." We worried. The wind whipped faster up there. The sun had set. The thermometer plunged. He finally came down for good and dated a girl who'd been my sister's bridesmaid and, as my sister told me, called her my name when he was drunk.

I couldn't go backward.

I sewed, making clothes from upholstery fabric because fabric at the dime store bored me. I was lonely in high school, having spent my previous spare time carrying deviled eggs to phone company potlucks, or hanging out with Rodney V. Meadow's mother, once driving eighty miles with her to see a masseuse for her migraines, and we'd sat side by side in portable saunas shaped like washing machines, our heads sticking out. Now I pretended high school was writers camp. But students talked about how they held liquor, not how they shaped paragraphs. I dated a boy who went to community college forty miles away, and he rambled in a way I didn't understand, either because he was tripping or he'd read Rilke. I made a bong in shop class, and I bought a baggie of pot, which my mother found. She opened the door to the bathroom where I floated in the tub, offended she'd walked in. She shook the baggie's contents over me like sage over a chicken in broth.

Then my wandering grandmother's husband had a heart attack in their kitchen, and she ran out the door to tell a neighbor. By the time the neighbor called an ambulance, my grandmother had keeled over, another heart attack. We went to the two-coffin funeral, with the God-fearing and ex-con offspring in the first pew on the left side, and my dad and his two brothers in the first pew on the right. I sat behind my father and uncles, their shoulders heaving, bloated, stuffed with memory. And I understood for the first time that if someone you love dies you have sadness, but if someone you love dies and you have unfinished quarrels—lost chances, love you skipped like a bus that left the station a long time ago—you have sadness, also helplessness and confusion.

The taskmaster grandmother came to celebrate my graduation. My mother bought me a typewriter for a gift. I'd go to college, she said. She also said to remember I was training for a job that would last only until I had children, though later I might work part-time, and it had to be a job that would move as my husband's job would move.

I'd spent the winter drinking, smoking pot, staying out until dawn. I understood hangover recovery better than most subjects. At my graduation party, there's a photo of me sitting on my taskmaster grandmother's lap, though I'm too big for this, and I'm wearing a dress I designed myself, trying to look like a flapper, wearing a brooch Rodney V. Meadow's mother gave me that belonged to her mother, a hillbilly flapper's brooch made of paste and tin, something Rodney V. Meadow's mother would never wear and I was welcome to it, she'd said. So I'm a flapper, except it's 1976. In the photo, my grandmother—who'd endured a rural flapper, her rival—looks proud. I stare at the cake, queasy.

I'd started dating another farm boy. I'd had sex hundreds of times already. But this was my second lover. "This can't be your second time," he said once, perplexed. "You're too relaxed. You move your hips like an expert." I clarified: "I didn't say it was my second time. I said you're only the second person I've ever had sex with." In turn, I didn't understand him, that his emotions had been activated. I'd been playacting since Kindergarten.

I also dated a boy who'd arrived for the summer and I liked him less than the farm boy. The tourist boy had the exotic whiff of places I'd never been. Yet I failed to tell the farm boy I was dating the tourist boy, and in a town so small people told the farm boy for me. He broke up with me. He said, "If you're seeing other people, and you're probably leaving for college, we should call it quits." I started crying. He shook his head. "Why are you crying?" I was thinking about the hours spent embroidering dish towels and pillow slips, the green fields dotted with wild mustard. Verdant meadows. Years. Misspent? I said, "I liked you." He said, "I liked you. But that's not going to fix this."

I already knew that the two weeks when everyone had shared notebooks and pencils and stayed up late talking about Keats and Emily Dickinson, about compromise and high hope, had been an idyll. Real college had football players, business majors, and—I'd been for a two-day orientation—dorms that, full-up, felt like barracks. I'd started to tip, one wheel spinning on airy prospects, the other grinding through mud. Both worlds would be inhospitable, one an aspiring place where I'd be an amateur all over again, uneasy, missing my set of instructions. Daydreaming would take me over. Teachers would misunderstand. Or I'd stay where I didn't fit, but I'd feel superior. Now which?

Regional Trades

When I was little, my mother had said to ignore the bars, though my brother and I once pressed our faces against the windows of one called the Chatterbox, which featured strippers. A day-drinker had lurched onto the sidewalk, blinking. A man in a white apron followed, yelling, "Kids, scram." Strippers took customers upstairs to bedrooms, we knew. Prostitutes also lived at the end of Main Street in the Depot Hotel, until it burned to the ground when one of them fell asleep while making a grilled sandwich on a steam iron. I assumed every Main Street had prostitutes and strippers. People need money, as my parents pointed out; these women had failed to acquire sensible vocational training. Meanwhile, my sister knew bookkeeping, and I, bad at math but good at spelling, knew stenography.

Except for a few years after Prohibition, the legal drinking age in Wisconsin had always been eighteen. Having finished high school now, I needed to choose my bar. Your bar, like your prom dress or favorite song, should match your personality. For instance, my dad would slip out of his store, past the Palace Movie Theater, and into the Corral, where the bartender had my dad's drink ready, a brandy Manhattan, also standing orders if my mom phoned and asked for my dad—she'd stopped phoning years ago—to say he wasn't there.

I sampled one drink at Railroad Memories, another at Diamond Lil's, then the Buckhorn. Finally, I chose the Sportsman's because I'd been in the apartment above it before I was old enough to go to the bar. During my senior year, I'd left school during lunch hour with a girl whose brother, Brock, had dropped out of college to work at a factory in Colorado, then returned to Wisconsin with his pregnant bride, Leila, who already had two daughters. Brock's father gave him the Sportsman's as a means of support and a place to live.

Brock and Leila filled the rooms with big floor pillows covered in batik. Brock lit a joint and passed it around as Leila's two daughters skipped past. I pondered this, then approved. If my parents drank in front of children, if everyone's parents did, why should these interesting newlyweds be hypocritical about a peaceful, herbal high? I watched to see what else was different, what chores and responsibilities. Would this marriage be co-constructed by the wife? Brock stared. He'd read my mind, maybe. I waited. He waved his hand and said, "In the future, you understand, this will all be accepted." He exhaled. "Pot."

Pot, then. So far, I'd smoked just at night, and I didn't like being stoned by day, the roar in my head as I went back to school, then work at the clothing store, then dinner with my parents and brother. Sitting in class and pretending to study, ringing up customers buying permanent-press slacks, eating while following family conversation turned complicated. Being stoned while not seeming stoned required strenuous exertion as I overcame obstacles, traversed sundry locales. To what end? Renewed gratitude for normalcy.

One evening, leaving work, I visited Brock and Leila. My sister was also a newlywed—her father-in-law had provided a small, remodeled house because there weren't suitable places to rent. My sister talked about carpet pile, upholstery swatches. And I'd grown up watching that TV show, Bob Eubanks sending Brylcreemed husbands offstage, then asking wives in minidresses where was the most interesting place they'd made whoopee. The studio audience liked couples who fought, swatting each other with answer cards. Brock and Leila spoke softly to each other—amused, not angry, if children drew on the walls. Leila's maternity dresses looked like a queen's, hems swishing the floor.

Downstairs the bar was full of post-hippies who'd started communes on farms they'd bought at rock-bottom prices. In far-off cities, punk and disco were already underway. But I didn't know. I pinned, snipped, and sewed paisley fabric into peasant blouses and graceful dresses. At a store on the edge of town that sold guns and fishing tackle, I bought a pair of moccasins that laced up to my knees. *Adventitious protective coloration. A creature's color and pattern will blend with the environs.* And so I spent Saturday nights talking to people ten years older than me who were for the barter system and against capitalist exploitation. Men wore bib overalls. Their girlfriends wore bib overalls too, with silky shirts. There were also the lone men, all with spade-shaped beards.

I met another married couple. The wife had feather earrings and a proud way of tilting her head when she spoke. She asked where I would go to college, what would I study. English, I said, at the small college eighty miles south, in Eau Claire. She told me to read Marge Piercy or, failing that, Sylvia Plath. Week after week, like a teacher checking on assignments, she asked me: had I read these writers yet? The public library didn't have them, so she loaned me her Marge Piercy books. One night she sat at a table and read aloud "The Implications of One Plus One," poetic cadences mingling with the plastic slap of Foosball. When she was done, she said, "Jealousy is an emotion I choose not to feel." Her eyes lingered on me. Her husband's eyes lingered on me. Did one of them want to sleep with me? I wondered. I decided I had the summer to figure it out and whether or not I believed in free love, which seemed philosophically akin to the barter system.

Sometimes I babysat Leila's children so Leila could spend time in the bar with Brock. When the girls were asleep, I was supposed to come downstairs for a beer and a bump. A bump was what people called a shot of whiskey or brandy or schnapps or Galliano. Infinite choices for bumps, I thought, surveying tiers of bottles in front of the mirror. Then one night the door swung open and a man stood there, a stranger-come-to-town, hero or villain, to be determined. Brock laughed, then climbed over the bar to hug him.

His name was Joe. Joe had ridden his motorcycle from Colorado. Then Brock started singing "Indiana Wants Me" and burst out laughing. When I asked Brock why, he explained that Joe was wanted in Indiana. I was wondering if it was polite to ask what Joe was wanted for, when Brock laughed again and said: "Don't worry. He's no ax murderer." Something political? I thought. Joe had protested social injustice? Joe had the Sir Galahad hairstyle most men had—our pastor, the young tenor on *The Lawrence Welk Show*. Maybe Joe's hair was trendy. Or a sign of allegiance to reformers who'd hoped to fix America, first by revolution, then by organic farming. Or he couldn't afford a barber.

Another detail I tried to decipher was that he wore sunglasses at night. He took them off and squinted at me. I must have squinted back. Brock explained that Joe had lost an eye in a BB gun mishap when he was a kid. "I see you're not wearing your eye patch," Brock added, jovial. Joe threw his hands in the air, his signature joke-delivery gesture, grinned at me, and said, "I save it for special occasions—weddings, funerals, whatnot."

What I later learned to call social mores were in a state of flux. A line had once separated people who went to strip joints from the rest of us. Now, partly because of the U.S. president who'd resigned for being a crook, and new attitudes about poverty, sex, and money, outlaws seemed like truth-speakers and insiders like colluding frauds. "Every place has strippers and prostitutes," a man with a spade-shaped beard said. "Strip clubs on Main Street are uh, uh, un . . . not hypocritical." He'd had a stutter when he was young.

Also, if somebody wanted to have sex with me and I wasn't interested—this had happened with the tourist boy—he could say I had hang-ups, whereas in the past I could have acted virginal, offended. And if I'd known what social class is—and you don't until you leave the class you're in, and Spooner had clique gradations anyway, not class gradations, because there wasn't wealth, not even post–civil rights economic segregation either, just all-white, rural sameness in which people paid attention to minute status markers like whether someone put paneling in their basement and made it into a den or left it full of cobwebbed junk, or how recently someone repainted their barn—I'd have seen that the just-arrived post-hippies were upper-middle-class and living with townies who'd grown up hardscrabble and preferred communes because now people with money helped do chores.

Joe had grown up hardscrabble. His mother died when he was young. Suicide.

She ate rat poison, Leila told me later.

One day Joe and I were sitting at the end of the bar, and the woman who'd gone to Vassar and wore feather earrings walked past; her husband had on a straw hat like a scarecrow's. When they were out of earshot, Joe said: "People who have advantages and pretend they don't are still phony." Maybe educated people intimidated Joe. Maybe he intimidated them. "Alienation schmalienation," he said. "Nobody likes work. Of course local yokels like a commune," he added. "Less work, more food, interesting sex just down the hall." I protested. "They have ideals. They want a life that's . . ." I paused. "Egalitarian."

On the other hand, the bar wasn't egalitarian.

Once I played "Theme from *A Summer Place*" on the jukebox. One of the men with beards—this one had a beaky nose—objected, moving his barstool near mine until his thigh pressed against my thigh. He told me that the Percy Faith Orchestra was an ersatz copy of real orchestras playing real art, which never lulls its audience into complacency. Joe liked the J. Geils Band, which wasn't on the jukebox. Joe probably didn't like "Theme from *A Summer Place*" either. Yet he interrupted and said: "Okay, it's not about peace, love, dove, and incense. But you can listen without losing your grip."

So I mostly sat with Joe, who didn't harp about what I didn't know, because he didn't know either. I told him that the woman with feather earrings had loaned me books. "Maybe I don't understand them," I said, "but they seem full of advice, correct thinking, and that gets old no matter how nice the word choice is." The correct thinking was feminism, of course. I wasn't a feminist, not yet, though in time experience would teach me to be. But even by then I'd never like poems that seemed more edifying than beautiful. So far I liked Keats—whose poems about love as the meaning of life until you get clued in that death trumps love—amazed me. And I'd found a book of Richard Brautigan's poems at the Rexall Drug. They weren't reliably interesting, but the slangy style was a good example because I hadn't been anywhere besides Spooner. Did Joe like poetry?

He said, "If you do, Queenie."

But he didn't like Leila. She'd had her baby now and gazed at it tenderly as she yanked her dress aside for feedings. Joe had known her years. "She was about to be evicted with children," he said. "Then she spotted Brock. Some guys will fall in love with their first lay. She's been looking for a meal ticket since day one." I argued that raising children was work, that she bartended. Joe pointed out that Leila went downstairs to be in the bar, not work. She didn't cook or clean. It was true that the dirty dishes in the kitchen were glasses, cups. The trash overflowed with carry-out containers from the Topper Cafe. Joe stayed in the spare bedroom and cleaned the kitchen every day. Or I did.

Leila had to come upstairs every three hours to breastfeed. One night, I held the baby until she slept, then put her in her basket. The girls, who'd moved the TV into their bedroom, dropped off. Then Joe leaned over and kissed me: slow, luxurious. I thought the sex would be luxurious too. But Joe didn't know—not in the way that Rodney V. Meadow had known—what I liked. I reminded myself that Rodney V. Meadow and I had learned to do for each other over time. How long had it taken? I couldn't remember. I'd been so sure of Rodney I used to tell him exactly this, that. My time with Rodney had been like marriage, I realized—doctor's appointments, shared holidays. But I couldn't go back.

When Joe was done, he lay next to me. In nearby rooms, the children breathed softly. Jukebox thumps rose though the floor. Neon light from a bar across the street blinked against the windows. Joe said,

"This is as close as two people get." Of course he knew that people who weren't close had sex, but this was the poetry he had. When Leila came upstairs, we were dressed but holding hands. "God," she said. "I blame myself."

One day, Joe and I were taking the children to the town playground. I'd packed a lunch—sandwiches, chips, cans of root beer. I put the baby in a backpack carrier. Joe toted the picnic and a brocade bag with diapers and bottles of the formula Leila had begun using because, between months of pregnancy and nursing, she was tired of not drinking.

We left the apartment and headed down Main Street, past bars, past the dime store, past the Palace Movie Theater, and a woman my mother knew drove by. Her steering turned erratic as she craned her neck to see me carrying a baby, walking with a man who looked not only too old but, by her measure, like a drug addict or low-class hobo, not to mention the school-age children prancing. She simplified this tableau when she called my mother, pretending to chat about altar flowers, then saying, "Debbie had a baby?"

My mother recounted this conversation that night. She'd said I hadn't had a baby, no. I was clerking at the clothing store and babysitting too. "But whose baby is it?" she asked me.

"My classmate's brother's," I said. "His wife already had the other children."

"You babysit for fun, not pay?" I nodded. "Then why were you alone with the father?"

"That's their friend," I said. "He lives with them."

"In a commune?"

If I said yes, I could imply there was an etiquette she didn't understand—shared activities, outings. Or I could tell the truth and say Joe was staying there until he found a job. But this would let her know Joe was my boyfriend and she'd ask to meet him. I was raised to be a farmer's wife, a shopkeeper's wife, a telephone man's wife. Joe would seem all wrong, past thirty with no regular job. Shiftless, she'd think—lacking resources to shift for himself and me. I said, "A small commune, yes."

But before I fielded her questions, Joe and I got to the park. I held Leila's baby. The girls ran—happy, shrieking—to the seesaw. Then I noticed Joe had his face in his hands. I thought he felt sick. He sat up, took a bandanna out of his pocket and wiped his forehead, then his one eye. Let me emphasize that a missing eye isn't symbolic. I'd once had a kind teacher who lost an eye to cancer, no connection to Joe, who lost his in an accident. Having loved two people with missing eyes isn't the key to my character as I proceeded in life, a competition in which the object is the most progress with the least misery.

Joe cleared his throat. He had a daughter named Josie, he said. When he was at work one day, his wife moved back in with her parents. Joe never saw Josie again, except in a restaurant with his wife's father watching. "He was kind of a nabob locally—glad to get rid of me. I'd have needed money for a better lawyer than his." Joe went to Kokomo to look for work. Then a friend from Colorado called about a factory with good wages. Joe paid child support on time for three years. Then the factory laid off, rehired, laid off. Last year his cousin had called and said there was a warrant for his arrest in Indiana.

"I can't go back there," Joe said, unconsciously quoting the song.

In Brock's inebriated moments he'd sometimes do the end of the song, when police say: "You're surrounded. Give yourself up." I asked Joe if he hated Brock's singing. Joe said, "He's just keeping it light—he understands I made miscalculations that snowballed."

The phrase "deadbeat dad" didn't exist yet. So I didn't have an automatic way to say it was wrong Joe's daughter didn't know her father. Or that, to get by, Joe's ex-wife had to live off her father. But if Joe was telling the truth, he'd need money to float like a miracle from the sky, also one of those kindly judges from an old-time movie who'd see that Joe had been railroaded out and needed a way back. Joe hadn't known his father—not even a name. Here he was, helping with Leila's baby, not his, who must be as old as the girls now. They ran to the swings; I called for them to be careful. I tried to see Joe's story in a skeptical light. Was this why he'd objected to Leila? He felt like a meal ticket?

Joe said, "I just want to make it right."

I pictured his return—getting out of a car at sunrise, a determined look on his face.

"When I do," he said, "I'll take you with me."

So there'd be a stepdaughter I'd learn to love. I pictured myself in an airport somewhere, pushing a stroller. Would this be my baby? It couldn't be Leila's. I'd wear a filmy dress, silver earrings; Joe would look better too. I'd buy him new T-shirts. I wondered if I'd like him to wear the eye patch. I would, I thought, if we were far from Spooner.

This was my playground daydream.

I left for college in two weeks.

Once renowned for twenty-two sawmills, Eau Claire had a little university, a tire factory, a brewery that made bad beer, and a toilet paper factory that pumped gray dross into a sludgy peak. Most students came from Milwaukee suburbs, I gathered, and bought their school clothes at department stores. Some had received new cars for high school graduation gifts. I met kids from small towns too, yet I didn't get to know them because they didn't talk in class. I got Bs and Cs on my assignments. I had a bad moment in Intro to Philosophy when we discussed collective moral standards, and I raised my hand to ask how it's possible to know morality from immorality in a purely theoretical context, though I didn't have the right words to ask my question like that. The professor turned scathing.

I walked off campus, exploring the tiny city. Every few blocks, I found a new business district with a one-room grocery, tailor, florist, shoe repair, and tavern. One corner had four houses with cupolas and stained glass windows, built in the 1920s—each a wedding present from a lumber baron to one of his four daughters, the historical marker said.

Temperatures dropped.

I stopped wearing my dresses with moccasins and wore jeans, flannel shirts, and Red Wing work boots. One day, as rain turned to sleet, I realized that if I continued using the Hunting & Fishing Supply as my shoe store, I'd need felt-lined rubber boots next. Then I headed back to the dorm, where girls played Peter Frampton and hot-rolled their hair.

One night I put a fan in my window facing out, lit a joint, and blew the smoke outside. In the morning, I found a note on my door with shapely Magic Marker letters: "Stop being a DOPE." Now I truly didn't fit. A pretty girl one day asked me—a small troupe of her friends listening—why I never spent weekends at the dorm. Instead of giving her a complete answer, I said: "I visit my boyfriend." She asked where he went to college.

He's thirty-two," I said. "He doesn't think about college."

In fact, I went north every weekend because my mother and father had arranged trips—my mom's a guided tour with my taskmaster grandmother, my dad's a fishing trip to Alaska—but neither had told the other before the nonrefundable down payments got made.

I couldn't keep straight who'd been rude first and who'd retaliated. My dad's trip preceded my mother's, but he wouldn't have taken his if she hadn't been greedy and set up hers, but before that he'd ignored their silver wedding anniversary. So I came home to cheer up my mother. Then she left, and I came to clean for my dad and brother. I'd see Joe at night. He had a job at the boat factory in Shell Lake. He'd drive over to see me in a car he'd traded his motorcycle for. We babysat for Brock and Leila, who weren't getting along either.

I should have tried to make friends at school. But one day, as I looked for rides to Spooner on a bulletin board called the ride board, I found a steady ride to Shell Lake. A guy who stayed on someone's couch on weekdays, then went to Shell Lake on weekends, picked me up on Friday and took me back on Sunday. Joe had told me about his place. A woman cleaned the bathroom every day. This confused me. Why just the bathroom? What did "place" mean? Was this an idiomatic tic like saying "soda" instead of "pop," or calling me Queenie, which I'd heard only for dogs, not girlfriends? When I got there, I understood. He lived in a room above a bar and shared a bathroom with people down the hall.

He looked scruffy. After he washed up and changed into a fresh T-shirt and better jeans, I could see why, when he was young, a nabob girl in his high school had loved him. But he didn't like cleaning up. We argued. I wanted him to put his best foot forward. He said he'd stopped believing a best foot forward mattered.

One weekend, we drove to Spooner to visit Brock and Leila, who were moving into a house. Brock's dad was redecorating the apartment because it needed to bring in money to cover the house payment. Joe and I went back to Shell Lake and walked the shore of its namesake lake, which I knew as a place to swim and frolic. I'd never seen it in winter, its grim expanse crisscrossed by snowmobile tracks. We ate at a café, though Joe kept food in his room, including perishables between the window and screen. One night, we lay in bed, a streetlight shining around the curled edge of a window shade. Joe said he'd move back to Colorado after Christmas. The factory was hiring. I pictured a conveyer belt. I said, "In political science, we discussed minimum wage, the treadmill life."

"So on and so forth. I can't stay here." Joe gestured at the room.

Then one night at school someone banged on my dorm room door. I opened it. Life had shifted again, but I didn't know how yet. A girl from the dorm said, "This is an emergency."

My sister and her husband had been driving to a store in a town named Rice Lake—its lake is bigger than Shell Lake, the town named after its lake is bigger too. My mother had told them not to go, icy overpasses. But, adults now, they made their own decisions.

They were alive, in ambulances en route to an ICU in Minneapolis. My mother arranged for a friend of a friend's son to drive me to Minneapolis. When I got there, I stumbled through the hospital, asking strangers for directions. My mother's face said hello. Then a nurse's face said it would be difficult to see my sister. My mother blurred and disappeared into the waiting area. My dad, I don't remember, but he must have been there, my brother too. My sister sat propped in bed. She chanted rhymes, her bandages like a turban. She called me baby names, and we were preschoolers again, inseparable, speaking a private language. Except I was the big sister now. I whispered not to say certain things—she was talking about bathroom functions. "Not that," I scolded.

I stepped outside.

The nurse said, "The brain is like Jell-O. It got shook up. It takes time to settle again."

I cried hard in the nurse's station. Then stopped crying.

I went back to school. I was behind in my homework.

I pushed bad thoughts away. Or I wasn't old enough to wonder if the injury was permanent. My mother and the doctor kept the prognosis sunny. "She'll be fine in a few months." My dad might have worried she wouldn't be, but his duty was work, not family.

Marriage lasts in sickness and in health, especially during sickness because it's impossible to make a change. My sister and her husband left the hospital and went to my parents' to convalesce. They had matching wheelchairs, my mother said by phone.

When I got home in December, having handed in my last final, my father was remote, my mother fake-perky. My sister—her concussion rehabilitation underway—was unusually glad to see me. Wires stuck out of her husband's temples, plastic tabs on the ends so people wouldn't get scratched. "Doctors will cut those wires off lickety-split," my mother said. "And," she added brightly, "please invite your friend Joe for Christmas dinner." Someone she knew had seen me with Joe, walking the streets of Shell Lake. I told her not to worry: "He'll be moving back to Colorado." She said, "Just invite him. No one should be alone on Christmas."

Around noon, Joe arrived in his banged-up car.

An old car is fine, my dad would tell you. God knew he wasn't a snob, he'd say, having come from nothing. But the old car shouldn't have rust, dents, dings, missing chrome. It should be glossy with wax. Joe stomped snow off his shoes as I opened the door.

My dad leapt out of his La-Z-Boy and said, "Where's your home, son?" My mother rolled her eyes. My dad had shifted into this father-who's-protecting-defenseless-daughter mode we'd never seen before. I know now, if I didn't then, that Joe scared him: Joe's age, Joe's size, his unfamiliar ways. Joe said, "Indiana, sir."

Joe wore a sports coat I'd never seen—I found out later it belonged to the son of a woman he'd worked with at the boat factory. He had on a new shirt, wrinkles still visible from where it had been folded in cellophane. If this were my dad's shirt, new but not ironed, my mom would call it tacky. But I could tell by the look on her face she felt tenderhearted that Joe had tried to dress up for us, sad, too, that he was my boyfriend. He was freshly shaved. His hair looked shiny. I'd warned my mother he'd lost an eye. In a poised way, she was inspecting his face now. Until you got close, he looked like someone who'd been outside a lot, sun creases. He was rough-hewn but handsome when he wasn't coming off the end of his shift with fiberglass stuck to his clothes.

My mother had bought him a gift. He thanked her and unwrapped it, Avon soap on a rope. He hung it around his neck. "It fits," he said, standing up and throwing his hands in the air. My sister's eyes widened. "I like him," she said. "He's funny!" She was at the stage of recovery when she blurted. Yet everyone was so happy she was talking at all, even if what she said was uncharacteristic, that we all laughed, cozy group-laughing.

A few days later, Joe left. "Queenie, it's been sweet."

I wasn't exactly sad.

We'd hit an impasse.

I started to plan my life. I wanted out of the dorm: the competing stereos, hairdryers, chatter; girls with winged hairdos, winged sleeves on their blouses, winged shins on their pants.

I stayed home and applied for jobs. I sewed new clothes. I bought women's shoes at the store where I used to work. The clerk who'd replaced me waited on me, silent. My former boss kept his distance. I'd disgraced myself, it seemed. I practiced my shorthand and went on interviews at county and state bureaus. "Few people know shorthand these days," a man who interviewed me said, approving. But a stenographer with experience got hired, not me.

The man called a few days later to say he'd found me a job, due east, near the border of Michigan's UP. My mother urged me to take the job, describing benefits, transfers. Yet I couldn't bring myself to move deeper into the pine woods. My dad told me to join the army. "You like going places and . . ." he paused, "meeting unusual people. You'll get job training besides." My mother said to get waitress experience. "You'll use it all your life."

One night she called me to the phone.

When I picked up, Joe said, jolly, ironic: "Queenie?" I tried to picture him in Colorado, but I'd never been there. "Hello," I said, puzzled. We hadn't pledged to be in contact.

He lowered his voice and said I should come. He missed me. He'd gotten a promotion. "I have a room in a house. Not like you think. I share a house with friends and their ten-year-old son. You can drive me to work and use my car to look for a job." I told him I'd think about it. I hung up and saw the wary look on my mom's face. But ads for nearby jobs had dried up. I decided to go to Colorado. I wouldn't be the first or last woman to use a man as a way to leave home, and sometimes you go sideways or down before you go up. All Joe expected was loyalty, maybe cooking. I asked my mother to drive me to the airport in Minneapolis. She said no.

But when I started checking Greyhound schedules, she changed her mind. Only if I'd buy a round-trip plane ticket, she said. I wasn't coming back, I said. She said leave the return date open—I'd come for a visit. I bought the ticket, using money from savings. These were days when people walked passengers all the way to the gate and waved as the plane lifted off. As we crossed the parking lot, snowflakes drifted down and melted on my mother's face. When I turned to go, she looked smudged. I got on board.

I remember Colorado Springs as buildings beside a snow-spackled ridge of mountains. I drove Joe to his factory with its big sign: HIGH ALTITUDE. LOW HUMIDITY. BEST METAL WORK IN THE USA. I never saw the inside. Joe came home every night, filthy. I'd packed clothes for job interviews, yet no ads asked for stenographers. My typing was an asset, but I didn't interview well; I was eighteen. I'd never worked anywhere except the clothing store. I applied at clothing stores, and people taking my application were older, strikingly attired. Joe talked about getting me on at the factory. As days dragged, I learned to make potato soup, macaroni with cheese called rat trap, more potatoes, hamburger, kielbasa. When our housemate's ten-year-old got in from school, we walked to the grocery store, and I'd have dinner ready when the adults came home.

I spent time with the ten-year-old because conversation was easy—how teachers make you feel, what TV shows we liked. I avoided his parents' friends who came and went. Joe's housemates and friends used pot, alcohol, but also mescaline and downers to make weekends special. Joe liked just alcohol and sometimes cheap speed.

One nice weekend Joe and I drove to Cripple Creek to visit his friend who worked in the mines and had married a woman with a baby. In the evenings, the men drank beer while the woman fed the baby, then crocheted. She gave me yarn and a hook so I could crochet too. One night she made tuna casserole. When I said it was good, she said she'd added sour cream for extra flavor, and I nodded, impressed at culinary improvisation. Her husband said that the mine's better pay meant better grub, this nightly reminder of affluence, and I thought for a minute about the piddling cost of a carton of sour cream. But I let my snobbish thought go because I liked these people. Then Joe and I went home.

Most weekends we went to a bar called the Wagon Wheel. Joe wore Levi's, a black T-shirt, his leather eye patch. I'd put on my Saturday night best—lace mixed with denim, earrings made of beads and chips of deer antler. One night a man who was tripping or jacked up on white cross spoke to me. I answered politely, and he pulled a knife. Joe knocked him to the floor, then dragged me out of the bar. He said, "Queenie, you need to learn to tell good from bad." We were on Joe's turf now. One night we were making love, and Joe said, "Virgins are overrated." I turned away. "I was not a virgin when we met. If you want facts, you lack finesse too." He sighed. "We were kidding, right?"

One day I had a toothache and spent almost the last of my money on a dentist who used gas. So far, I'd had only Novocain. The dental assistant put a mask over my nose and said, "Is it enough yet? Is it enough yet?" I winced at the tooth, the dentist prodding, and shook my head no. Then I fell backwards and down. I found my dad and Joe in a hole. Why had I never noticed that they were alike? Their whiskers were coming in as five o'clock shadow, and both of them said I'd never understand. My mother leaned over the top with a woman dressed in white, and light was brighter there. I must have had no better way to sort this out than Sunday school imagery: "There is a hell?" I said. The dental assistant, in white, removed the gas mask. "Oops," she said, "too much."

One Sunday morning, the phone rang. Someone rapped on our bedroom door. "Telephone call from Wisconsin," the ten-year-old yelled. Hungover, I dressed to take the call. "Hello," my mother said in that fast and formal voice she used for long-distance, expensive minutes ticking away. She had my dad pick up on the extension. He said hello in a too-neutral voice. She asked what I'd been up to. I told her about new foods I'd cooked, that I'd had a toothache. She listened, then asked, "When are you coming home?" I said, "I'm waiting for a job at the factory." She said, "No. Call the airline and get a flight. I'll call back tonight, and you'll tell me exactly when to pick you up." Maybe it was the staying home every day, waiting for a ten-year-old's return and then Joe's. Or it was my mother's stern tone—as if I were ten. I obeyed.

In early April—thaw, freeze, snow, thaw, freeze, snow—I'd wake in my old bedroom, put on a black uniform with white diamond shapes on the bust and hips meant to amplify female contours, then my coat, hat, gloves, and walk past clapboard houses, then down Main Street to the Topper Cafe. In the morning, I served eggs and bacon; for lunch, hot beef, fried liver. Every day, the most vocal of the grizzled men who sat at the counter asked if I'd bend over the cooler another time. Or stick my finger in his coffee to make it sweet. The other men chortled. The first guy would say, "You should move to Las Vegas. No use sitting on that money-maker." I worried my job with its self-display, the striding across the café in my sex-robot waitress suit, signified changed status. "Are you friends with my dad?" I'd ask, changing the subject.

The first Saturday I went back to the Sportsman's, Brock rushed around the bar to hug me, to ask how Colorado was. I answered that Colorado was nice—though I'd seen just glimpses. I said Joe and I didn't talk often because long-distance cost too much. Brock started singing "Indiana Wants Me" robotically, as if he'd forgotten why he'd sung it in the first place. He was out-of-his-gourd drunk, I realized. One of the men with beards, the stuttering one, told me Leila had taken the children and moved in with a commune-dweller, but not at the commune. Where were they? He shrugged. I thought about the children. Would Brock see them again?

I sat next to the woman with feather earrings. Even one semester at a regional college will improve your small talk—I'd read Sylvia Plath. "Better yet," I added, "John Berryman." John Berryman's poetry was gorgeous but bewildering, a line here or there making my heart thrill, a whole poem beyond me; I wasn't a good enough reader yet. She said, "Another male poet, great." I said, "But John Berryman *is* great. He's better than Marge Piercy." She stared at me. Commune-dwellers, or housemates in Colorado, have the same pecking orders as people any-where, I realized. I resented my elders for having more choices, better ways of justifying choices, and they treated me like the amateur I was.

One night, the man with the beaky nose suggested we all go to the Chatterbox. He'd majored in economics. "Consider it research." An-other person suggested the new strip joint on the edge of town. The beaky guy argued for the Chatterbox. "It's historic." But everyone else wanted the new strip joint. One of the bib-overalled women smiled at me. "Let's go. It will be a lark."

We went to a one-story building that used to house an LP gas supply. We stared at the stripper's G-string and pasties. She went through the motions—thrust, spin, twirl, dip, spin. I studied her face. She looked like a store clerk, pleasant yet aloof.

One of the bearded men leaned over and told me that lipstick evolved as part of a female's mating display because red lips simulate the female state of arousal. Another shouted to the stripper: "Are you happy? Is this life fulfilling?" The one with the beaky nose took money out of his wallet. The woman who'd thought this visit to a strip joint would be amusing stared at the floor.

The stripper shook her hips, hands in a V-shape pointing to her privates, and she smiled at the regulars, who leered unapologetically. This was my hometown, schizophrenic. It had fragmented thinking. The post-hippies thought they were better than horny old-timers. Horny old-timers thought that they were no worse, for instance, than a bearded guy talking to a stripper about happiness sitting next to another holding a ten-spot near the stripper's crotch. Outside, all around us, in houses with lights turned down, furnaces humming—my sister and her husband had just moved back into their house, so recently remodeled it still smelled like paint—were people who'd married because sex felt like love, and the feeling sometimes lasts and sometimes doesn't.

I talked to Joe on the phone. "You're my bright spot," he said.

Weeks passed, and the owners of the Palace Theater came to eat lunch at the café. They'd refurbished the Palmote Drive-In too. Their names were Shelley and Bubbles, and they were ex-carnies. Everyone knew the Palace Theater on Main Street showed G-rated movies at seven p.m. and X-rated movies at nine p.m. Shelley buttered his dinner roll. "PG, which stands for 'parental guidance,' has replaced M," he said, "which used to stand for 'mature.' R for 'restricted' is always a possibility too. But movies like these have always flopped for me at the Palace," he added. "My core markets are families with kiddos and the single fellas."

Bubbles suggested I serve concessions at the drive-in on weeknights. Because I was a good waitress, she said. Flattery, yet another currency. The Palmote showed horror movies on weekends, I knew.

During the school year, if the thermometer stayed above zero and snow wasn't expected, a high schooler might drive through the gate with a keg in the back of his pickup—I'd gone a few times, milling, drinking, the beleaguered babysitters on the screen irrelevant. That day in the café I didn't think to ask Shelley and Bubbles what the Palmote played on weeknights. Weeknights, I watched TV with my parents, my dad snoring in the recliner. Or he'd stay at the Corral, and my mother would confide gloomily that she'd done her best, cooking, raising children, bookkeeping, having sex. "It pays minimum wage," Bubbles said. Spring was here, I thought. Ennui again. Longings. I decided to work two jobs, save for a car, move to a city, and wait tables there.

After work, I changed out of my uniform into jeans, a peasant blouse, my puka shell necklace, and I drove my mother's car to the Palmote. I passed the marquee that said XXX because Shelley was already waving me into a parking spot. Inside, he introduced me to Bubbles's nephew. "Bubbles wants Vinny to settle down with a local girl," Shelley said. I'd never seen anyone who looked like Vinny except in *West Side Story*, which I'd seen on TV. Vinny rolled cigarettes into his sleeve, passé. He had tattoos, also passé. Or not yet reinvented. Only sailors and Hells Angels had tattoos then. Shelley showed me how to use the pizza oven, the popcorn popper, the till. He left to start the movie. Vinny stood so close I smelled his aftershave. He'd moved to Spooner because his parole officer made him live with family, he said. He took a pint of booze out of his pocket, and a condom packet fell on the floor. Years would pass before people would worry about AIDS. I thought the condom was Alka-Seltzer until I picked it up and handed it back to him. What next? Moans, sighs, gasps.

On the screen, a man traveling in a foreign country got separated from his wife. In a tent filled with naked women, he fingered one set of nipples, then another. Porn stars don't seem real, I thought. Then— odd, creeping—that ancient sensation, arousal. Unsimulated. Maybe my lips were red. My arousal mixed with shame. It turns out I'm a bit of a prude. The so-called sexual revolution might have made me able to maintain a detached facial expression while college-educated people discussed free love, but I felt alarmed, then confused when the man on the screen plied various nipples. "Hmm," he said, "just like elevator buttons."

I quit, walking out the door.

When Joe phoned next, he said he was moving to Indiana. He wanted to come for me. I wondered: had he forgotten that I didn't know good from bad, that we'd worn each other down in close quarters? "Why are you quitting your good job?" I asked. "I've got money saved," he said. "It's now or never. It's all I know. Home."

I stalled. "Go straight to Indiana and get settled first."

He got mad. "You've met someone, is that it?"

The beak-nosed guy once swirled his hand on my back, but I'd walked away, blunt. The woman with the feather earrings had split up with her husband, and he'd turned out to be good-looking now that he'd taken off his straw hat—he had a dry sense of humor and twinkly eyes. If I stuck around, I thought, I'd head that way.

Joe said, "If you see me in person, you'll change your mind."

It was May when I drove the 1966 Pontiac Catalina my dad had found for me in a widow's garage—ten thousand miles on the odometer, no dents or dings—and I parked at the end of a driveway leading to a cabin that belonged to the woman at the boat factory who'd given Joe her son's sports coat. Ceramic trolls sat in the yard. Flower pots on metal stands whirled in the wind. I saw Joe's car. Then the door to the cabin opened, and Joe stood on the steps, smiling, waving me in. The woman was at work, I knew. "Come out," I said. "It's a beautiful day." The sky was blue for the first time in months.

We walked toward each other. He opened his arms. I stepped into them, commodious, familiar. But when he kissed me, I felt like an actress, a good actress. I threw myself into the performance: lovers reuniting. If I didn't kiss him, how could I justify that I'd slept with him for almost a year? If I felt indifferent, I'd be careless, without caring. I'd prided myself on caring.

Before I knew it, we were arguing.

Joe said he'd paid for everything in Colorado. I said, "But I had over

45

$700 before I left Wisconsin and less than $50 when I came home." He said, "I must have spent three times that much, for our rent, for your food and your drinks." I said, "You asked me to come. I cooked and cleaned for us. I looked for work. I tried."

We stared at each other. He turned and walked back to the cottage.

I never saw him again.

A few weeks later, I moved to Eau Claire and rented a bedroom in a house. I took summer-session classes. I didn't have sensible vocational skills, so I waited tables. As I served coffee, sandwiches, burgers, I considered all the menial ways to earn a wage—Joe at the boat factory, Joe at the steel factory. My dad had eked his way forward, and he got mad whenever he tried to explain how hard it had been. And any idea I got from bar talk that people don't pay for free love vanished. I came home for a visit and, on Main Street, near the Chatterbox, I ran into the post-hippie who stuttered. He said Leila had left Wisconsin, and her boyfriend from the commune had hooked up with another guy's wife.

Everyone has aspirations, I realized. Women who choose one mate, then another. Prostitutes and strippers do. Aspirations don't make you special. One day, I stepped on an elevator in the only tall building on campus, and I understood I'd never again push elevator buttons without thinking of nipples. Underemployed people bored out of their minds wrote that line, I thought, going up.

On the Down-Low

Late one night when no one was home, I worked in the living room while playing a Laura Nyro record. A roommate who'd competed for her hometown beauty pageant by singing "Climb Every Mountain" came in, stared at my typewriter and wadded-up papers, turned down the volume, and said, "She sounds like a panting dog when she sings the chorus." I hadn't known this roommate, or any of them, when I moved into my summer sublease bedroom, temporarily bedecked with doilies, knickknacks, and photos of ancestors I'd found in my parents' attic. I'd found my taskmaster grandmother's pedal-pump sewing machine too. Creativity and ambition converged as an impulse toward self-presentation that seemed less like style than performance art—still unknown in the upper Midwest.

Besides jeans and leotards, I bought my clothes at thrift stores: spangled vests, bolero jackets, men's suit coats. I bought curtains and sewed them into dresses. I was trying to look good, better. Yet, except for a Swedish art professor who taught Watercolor II and praised my outfits, the attention I got was startled.

My roommates at the summer sublease were two or three years older than me, except Lana, who was my age, but she hadn't dropped out of college at Christmas. When she asked why I had and came back so soon, I tried out answers. "I wanted to see Colorado, and I got the chance." Lana frowned. "I needed to save to buy a car, so I can drive to a job and still attend class." Lana frowned. "I felt guilty getting an education without first understanding the lives of the proletariat." Lana looked stunned. "My sister was in a car accident, and I felt too sad to study." Lana's facial expression recast itself as sympathy.

So, for a summer, in the company of Lana, I was pitiable, and she was kind. She took me to parties at her boyfriend's. She introduced me. People said hello, then ignored me as music got loud. Besides beer, there'd be bong hits. I'd end up silent, an especially florid wallflower I thought one night, studying my dress's fern-and-blossom fabric. Then summer ended, and I needed a new place, a habitat where I'd be surrounded by my own kind.

In Biology of National Parks, a class with scads of students in it, the professor took roll every day, mangling my last name. At the time, it was Frigen, and people pronounced it *Friggin* or—afraid of sounding obscene—*Frygen*. My family said *Frigane*. In Spooner, everyone heard it before they read it and didn't mispronounce it. So I'd never thought about it as a liability until now. I corrected the professor each time. One day, drowsy because I'd waited tables the night before, I put my head down, and I heard the professor say, "The first purpose of color change in chameleons is social signaling. Camouflage is secondary." Then: "Hey, you with the weird last name, don't sleep."

The students laughed. I sat up, casual-seeming. When class was over, I put my book in my backpack. I was wearing my last year's knee-high moccasins with a dress made from silky, golden curtains—I'd seen a photo of Stevie Nicks and admired the way she'd paired incongruous items, forging together the alien and separating the familiar, as Nietzsche said, though he meant we should disrupt word clichés, not fashion clichés. Still, I felt like I was in grade school. I chewed the inside of my cheek, worrying. In a few subjects, I got As and didn't know why. In others, I got low Cs and didn't know why either.

"Debra Frigen." *Frigane*. I looked up. A boy towered over me. "James Stillman here." He held out his hand, but I couldn't shake it because I was adjusting straps on my backpack.

"You moved here last June," he said. "I saw you."

I nodded. I didn't say that I'd moved here for the second time.

I didn't think much about him as I walked to my mustard-colored house by a swampy lake. He was tall, handsome, but his eyes looked like they belonged to a trapped animal.

I was busy—my typewriter and folder of poems, my classes, my job, my life at the mustard-colored house where I shared a room with a girl named Maribel. In August, the view from its window had reminded me of adolescence: solitary days running a boat along a peaceful shore. But there was nothing solitary about a house with five renters, though it wasn't fancy like the summer sublease, which I couldn't have afforded during the school year, so I might just belong with these new room-mates, I'd told myself. Besides, in a college town, good leases turned over in an annual wave—not much else had been available. We all contended with chronic unrest over who did or didn't do dishes, who'd eaten someone's TV dinner, who'd had sex on the living room floor under a blanket with lights turned off and mood music playing, a cue everyone else in the house took.

Except Ellen, who was religious. She flipped on the light and witnessed the spectacle, coitus interruptus under a lumpy blanket, then shrieked with her back turned until the boy was gone, and called a house meeting no one would attend. I mostly sided with Maribel, who'd been under the blanket in the living room because she didn't want to lock me out of our room. Ellen, who'd signed the lease before the rest of us, had the biggest bedroom to herself—not that she'd have sex before marriage because her body was a temple, she said. Two girls named Paula, one from a farm, the other a cello player, weighed in. Farm-Paula rolled her eyes and said, "Lordy, I hope they used a rubber. One minute you're frisky. Next thing you've got a baby with crappy diapers." Cello-Paula said, "I personally couldn't have sex in a living room like Maribel, but Ellen needs to get laid."

I was waiting tables one night when my boss, Kristine, called me to the phone. "Debra!" she said, accented, authoritarian. She was German. She'd married an American soldier during the Allied Occupation. She had a daughter my age, but they argued because the daughter skipped work, no warning, to go to motocross races with a boy who wore Budweiser T-shirts. Kristine left the receiver uncovered and said: "It is a call from a boy!"

I must have looked surprised. No one called me. When I answered, James Stillman said he'd gotten my number from the campus directory, called my house, and one roommate said I was at work. He'd asked where. She and another roommate didn't know, but they found Maribel—brooding and burning incense in our room, I figured—who'd told him the Crosstown Café. James wanted to go out. I was thinking: Friday, Saturday. Tonight, he said. With Kristine listening I didn't feel I could say I didn't get off work until late and had class in the morning. I said I'd call him after work.

When I got home, Maribel, Farm-Paula, and Cello-Paula were waiting in the kitchen. Who was he? How did I know him? When I said he wanted to go out tonight, but it was late and I'd take a rain check, they objected, especially Maribel, who was in love, unrequited. "Not the first time he asks you, no," she said. "Be picky later." Farm-Paula: "We have our studies, and we have our real goal, boys." Cello-Paula: "I tend to agree with Maribel this time. What class is that important?" I balked. My hair smells like kitchen grease, I said. I'd wash it, and it would take an hour to dry. It was fifteen degrees outside. Maribel threw her hands up. "For God's sake, use a hairdryer. Catch a cold."

I called James Stillman. He gave me directions to his house.

When I got there, he said he'd been insistent on tonight because his roommates had gone to a concert in Minneapolis, and he'd likely never have the house to himself again. He uncorked a bottle, lit a candle, put a jazz record on. He preferred Hendrix-style guitar. "But it makes conversation difficult." He showed me his own guitars, erect like trophies in front of a lit aquarium. We sat facing this guitar-and-fish-tank tableau. I took off my coat. Maribel had insisted I forsake thrift store creations for jeans and her own best sweater, mauve, fluffy. "You look incredible," James said. "I thought you might."

James rolled a joint and said my boss seemed mean. I said no, she was nice, just strict, no phone calls. He asked about my roommates, the ones who didn't know where I worked, the one who did. I explained that I hadn't known them when I moved in. I'd be moving to a new house soon—I'd arranged for Maribel's friend to take my half-bedroom. During Christmas break I'd move to a house more rundown, but I'd have my own room. I didn't tell James I didn't know roommates in my new house either, that I'd never made friends. Though I'd dropped out for just a semester, according to papers I'd filed as I re-enrolled, I was already nontraditional, a student "with above-average financial stressors and potentially isolating life experience." James asked where my new house was. Around the corner, I said. "From here?" He smiled and set down the joint. He started kissing as if to send a message: he had technique, also ardor, but he'd hold back until I murmured yes.

Then the music stopped. James said it was cold—on the couch, outside. "Will your car even start?" It would, I said. If it wouldn't now, it wouldn't in the morning either, the coldest hour of the day. His face clouded up. "I don't know anything about cars. I don't even have a license." This was unprecedented. Public schools still taught drivers ed. Some people didn't have cars, but no one didn't have a license. I asked why not. He said, "My so-called troubled youth. But I'm not getting into that." He said I should sleep on the couch, and he'd go sleep in his room. Because I'd been drinking, he added, kinder. He pulled blankets off his roommates' beds, heaped them on me, and went upstairs.

When dawn came through the window, I went outside and let my car idle as I scraped frost off the windshield. People were driving to work in rows, their faces calm, brains freshly rinsed by sleep. Then the front door to the house banged open, and James shivered on the porch, bare-chested, disheveled. "Call me tonight after you get home from your whatever." His voice echoed in the hush. A bundled-up girl walking past, book bag over her shoulder, glanced at me, then away. I went to class. But first I went to the mustard-colored house to get my textbook. Maribel said my morning return meant that I belonged to James Stillman now. "From here on," she told me, "your attention is divided."

My Intro to Communication professor said, "After you see these pie charts, the reason for reciprocity in self-disclosure will hove into view." A few days later: "I never appreciated the importance of Uncertainty Reduction Theory until a conversation with a colleague finally hove it into view." This professor's verbal tic and systematic enthusiasm about why we divulge intrigued me. But I got a D on my first paper, in which I wrote that that how we talk, act, and look is communication, and we change according to who we meet, becoming the person the other person wants. The professor said I was describing Accommodation Theory with semiology larded in, but none of this was on the syllabus.

More puzzling, I was getting a D- in Freshman English, though I was almost a second-semester sophomore. I went to Dr. Darden Stoat's office hours to ask why. In the spectrum of professor appearances, he was well groomed as opposed to, for instance, a history professor who wore the same pair of pants hooked at the waist with a paper clip for an entire semester. I spoke to Dr. Darden Stoat—Uncertainty Reduction Theory put to use. How was he? He hated the North. He hadn't pictured himself at a small state college. Did he have suggestions for improving my papers? He pointed at me. "You digress. But your digressions ultimately pertain. But this scenic route wearies me because I'm busy when I read." He described the term paper. "It will make or break you."

I worried about this paper in my new room that sometimes felt lidless—open to the infinity of ideas, best, worst. Train noises muffled the sound of roommates on the stairs. I'd hear a female giggling, stumbling, more footfalls, male voices. This would be the theater major who sometimes spent the night with two gay men. She slept naked except for pearls, she'd explained, though she was a virgin. Another roommate looked like David Bowie and sat in her room listening to David

Bowie while crying—I'd asked why, and she'd cried harder and said she couldn't tell me. I scrubbed the bathroom, though not the kitchen, preserved museumlike in a state of squalor that predated my arrival.

I saw my room as my apartment: apart. But once in a while I came through the front door and, before going upstairs, gazed at the parlor— its upright piano with carved grapes, the colored glass in panes around windows facing the river, a divan from the Jazz Age. James lived a half-block away now, and I tried to picture him here, sipping tea. I sat down. Dust rose in a puff. The front door opened, and one of my roommates scurried past.

I juggled my job, homework, and James. Our mutual regard had surged, wariness too. Regard + wariness = hope forcing its way through gloom toward light. *Call*: I love you. *Response*: I love you too. I'd had this exchange with my mother, less often with my father. Rodney V. Meadow and I said it. Joe and I did. In courtship, the male initiates it. James choked out his part after we'd had sex, increasing the odds that I'd reciprocate because he was virtuoso. Besides homework he read less than he should, he read *High Times*, *Guitar Player*, and *Playboy*, which—say what you will—informed a slew of men who otherwise would never have known that women have orgasms, a subtle way of arriving at them.

James had practiced on acquaintances, none of whom he'd loved, he said. He knew better than I did that delay, a perfectly timed pause, and then another, made fulfillment more intense. I was a host of emotion. I felt self-conscious, grateful, rattled, languid, necessary. What phrase covered this? I said *I love you too*, though I'd lately told myself in my room, staring at the ceiling, the unpredictable future, to say so carefully this time.

One night I'd dallied too long with James before I went home. My Sacco and Vanzetti term paper was due the next day. I'd Xeroxed microfiche newspaper articles from 1919 to 1927 and circled words used by reporters that suggested presumptions about guilt or innocence— the paper's gist. I'd tried not to dwell on old photos: Sacco's and Vanzetti's doomed faces; hysterical mobs that wanted Sacco and Vanzetti dead. But, reminding myself to avoid digressions that pertained yet wearied, I'd postponed writing. The theater major was out, I ascertained. My other roommate was listening to David Bowie.

I'd have to write the whole paper now or go to school and beg for an extension—uncertain outcome. Writing now was risky too. I sometimes got late-night brain static, worry in the form of freeze-frame images: authority figures with stern faces. As a child, I'd lie awake thinking that ghosts of people who'd died in our house just before we bought it were mad about renovations. Deferentially, I never touched the banister, the only surface not replaced or refinished. My mother would wake to find me standing over her as she slept. Worried, she took me to a doctor who'd prescribed yellow Valiums, children's Valium. My dad had the big blue ones. My mother dosed me once, then shuddered and tossed the bottle out. That night in my rented room, I pictured Sacco and Vanzetti, looking sad about their trivial afterlife as a Freshman English paper topic. Finally, I put my coat over my winter nightgown, made a plan, and started typing. I read what I wrote, marked it up, retyped, read what I wrote, marked it up, retyped. Again, again.

Perfectionism I'd so far expended on poems. By nine a.m., I didn't have time for another draft, so I hurried to campus. Dr. Stoat said he'd grade our papers—quickly, he stressed—then confer with each of us in private. I handed mine in, avoiding his skeptical gaze.

A few days later, I went to see James. His GPA had dropped, but a trendy psychology professor with a ponytail would hypnotize him to study harder, a tactic that had worked in the past and would again, James said. James had come to college at age seventeen because his social worker persuaded the judge that self-betterment occurs at college, not in the juvenile justice system. First, James got a job at a campus cafeteria. He didn't like it, but it qualified him for a job at a sandwich shop, which was where he'd worked when he'd spotted me. Now he sold pot. This paid well and conferred status. Everyone he hoped to impress wanted some and kowtowed. When I arrived that night, one roommate after another greeted me, then departed. James and I sat in the living room.

The weather had rallied—spring's foreshadowing, its foreplay—and I was wearing a tropical skirt with a leotard and a pair of pricey boots my mother had bought when she'd visited, postulating that I didn't have a better house with better roommates because I didn't have better clothes. She also bought me underwire bras that made my torso statuesque, and a coat—not as warm as the Persian lamb coat I'd found at a thrift store.

I settled onto the couch, and a roommate named Bob Barr came back and asked James for a private confab. When James returned, he said Bob Barr wanted weed to take to a party, and James gave him some, free. "This new batch is good. I'd like to get the word out," he said, sounding like my dad trying to increase foot traffic at the auto parts store. Then: "Bob just gave you a compliment." Bob Barr was a short guy who once took first place in a contest for chugging beer. James said, "Bob said that when you first came in wearing your modern coat. . . ." I'd worn it because the temperature was in the forties. My expression must have changed. James proceeded carefully now, as if he'd read a book about how to encourage your girlfriend to make the most of her looks. "Bob said you always look good, but he didn't know how good until you got rid of the old lady clothes."

I thought about how to answer. "Like I dress for Bob Barr," I said.

James laughed. "But I like the new coat. And your sexy boots."

I didn't want to look like a beauty queen contestant, or a Bob Barr fantasy either. And I was on a budget—trying to seem as if I preferred carefully mingled cast-offs, the mishmash effect. But I didn't own a full-view mirror and got just blurred or fleeting glimpses. Now James had dropped a hint. I was feeling demoted when he showed me an ornately inked butterfly on a scrap of paper thin as insect wings. "Pretty," he said. "It's blotter."

I thought of the blotter my mother had put on her desk to keep pens from scratching the wood. James waited for me to react. I didn't know yet that love seesaws forever between regard for the other and wariness for the self (self-protection). I thought James and I would one day get to reciprocal poise, and I didn't want to lose face first. "LSD," he said. I rolled my eyes: "I know that." I didn't. But I didn't want to seem like Farm-Paula. James grew up in a real city, Milwaukee. He said, "So you've tripped then. In Spooner?" This seemed unlikely. I lied again and said, "Colorado." Mentioning my time in Colorado with an ex-boyfriend older than James gave me back my edge. James looked hurt as he pulled the butterfly into quarters. "Ink amount determines potency," he added. I didn't say no, because No is complicated. Besides, I thought, I had an easy day tomorrow, lunch shift at the Crosstown Café, then my appointment with Dr. Darden Stoat.

But having lied made the tripping harder, because later—when I looked out the window and saw short people trekking down a street daubed in yellow, yellow pools of light, the people carrying fishing poles, and I thought *would they really, in March?*—I couldn't ask James if he saw them too. If he didn't, if we weren't supposed to share the seeing, he'd know I was a first-timer. I'd have to retract my lie, and retractions are hard, harder still if you're tripping. I put my thoughts into formation. I gave my thoughts orders. James burst into laughter. "Look. Trolls who fish." But enough about later. Carpe diem. First, he made us sandwiches and said, "Of course, it takes an hour to get off."

I nodded, grim. How long would "off" be?

James said, "I don't know how coming down has been for you in the past, but I try to sleep. Coming down is as bad as getting off is good." An algebra of pleasure and penance, I thought. Pleasure's first spate passed through. Vines on my ultratropical skirt twisted in a way that seemed right for this room with wet air, aquatic décor, the cumulative effect of a bubbling aquarium with bright fish darting, guitars like Neptune's forks, and the lush tangle in the window, a houseplant called a dragon tree or corn plant. I held a cup of Red Zinger tea, and the last swallow was a pool surrounded by fronds stirring—a landscape in a cup, miniature and antic, like a snowstorm in a globe, except it was summer here—and James took it to the kitchen sink. We went upstairs and had sex, only amplified. Hours passed. "We've peaked," he said. Sensation crackled like heat-lightning.

He slept. I redirected bad thoughts, released good ones, but I got angry thinking that James liked me more in new clothes and didn't know how grueling the LSD had been, was. These thoughts jammed, proliferated, so I put on my clothes and modern coat and went home, the black sky getting thinner, letting in light. At home, I flipped through newspapers one of my roommates had left in a stack by the door. I found a story about the First Annual Tattoo Convention, with a dozen black-and-white photos, the finalists for the Most Beautifully Tattooed Man and Most Beautifully Tattooed Woman Contests.

I got scissors, cut out these photos, and taped them on the bathroom wall that I'd sometimes surmised needed a poster, pictures, something, and, using bits of newsprint, cut geometric figures to counter the photos. It made an interesting effect, this bathroom with its claw-foot tub, ancient sink, commode with tall tank and chain, ceiling covered by pressed tin, and now the wall with inky-paisley men and women framed by triangle and boomerang shapes. The sky outside was blue now, and I remembered my ordinary life—the Swedish professor who'd like this bathroom, I thought, just as he'd liked the doodling in my notebooks better than paintings I'd completed for class, and he'd asked me to major in art. The sun, all the way up, shone through a grimy window onto the wall, and I saw how crazy I'd been. I ripped it all down, took a bath and hurried to the Crosstown Café.

My mother had brought my bicycle in the car trunk when she'd visited. I rode it to work over slushy streets, thinking exertion would sweat out the last of the drug. Daylight was bright. Traffic droned.

I locked up my bike and went inside to eat the special: green beans dressed with Roquefort cheese, a pile of cold chicken and hard-boiled eggs. I contemplated Kristine behind the counter. I felt love and fear. She was sublime as she told me the old man who rented an upstairs room had been incontinent. "He needs not a room but family or a private clinic and he has neither, *nicht*." She also worried about the cook, who would do well to take a short stay in a sanitarium, Kristine felt. She was mad that a man who'd come last night for all-you-can-eat had wanted more twice. She'd asked him, "More which? More chicken? More dumplings?" Both, he'd answered. She'd given him a saucer with a half-dumpling and a wing. "I said, 'You might get indigestion. You watch it. You should lose weight for health!'" I laughed, but my laugh sounded loud, so I looked at the counter and pretended to write on a napkin.

Kristine said, "Debra, you are blushing. Just your ears. Red ears. Is it a fever?"

I didn't want her to see my eyes, windows to the soul, also dead give-away that someone is addled due to illegal drugs. I clocked in. During lunch rush, I didn't make mistakes. Then I cleaned up, and the man who washed dishes, lurching because one of his legs was shorter than the other, brought me a tub of clean silverware and twisted his ankle. The silverware flew, each piece a missile with a silver stream shooting behind it. I grabbed the dishwasher to keep him from falling and somehow caught pieces of silverware, knowing that any I didn't catch would need to be rewashed. Kristine clapped her hands, her cue for speed. She couldn't afford to keep us on the clock past two. I picked up the rest off the floor, washed and dried quickly, slipping spoons, knives, forks into assigned compartments, and these slow-moving pieces had thread-sized, tinsel-like tails.

I left, pedaling across town.

I saw myself in a plate-glass window, perched on my bike. I looked like the wicked witch in *The Wizard of Oz*. I'd unloosed my hair from its hairnet. I had on my uniform and white shoes. My coat flapped behind me. The hardest part about doing drugs was the acting-upon-acting, I decided. Stone-cold straight or sober, I acted: trying to be who Kristine believed I was, who my roommates hoped to live with, who the girl would be that belonged to James. My self that I preferred stayed underneath those facets, each facet angled to please a different person. *To thine own self be true.* Polonius, you windbag, I thought. People would fire me, fail me. I hurried up the stairs of Hibbard Hall and sat in Dr. Darden Stoat's office. I said: How are you? I thought: How am I?

I worried that, apart from not passing Freshman English, I might have recurring, small-scale hallucinations forever. Probably not, though. Most people who drop acid don't turn out like the legend of Art Linkletter's daughter, I thought. Dr. Darden Stoat's beard was shiny as sealskin, and he rubbed it, stalling. So I'd fail, I thought. One fail would be like getting that first small dent in my car. Now I could relax in school. I longed for my car next. Why had I been bicycling in winter? Why was I still wearing this waitress suit, my hair an unkempt snarl? I could do with a short stay in a sanitarium, I thought, missing Kristine. All my selves felt jumbled, not separate like forks, knives, spoons.

Dr. Stoat said, "I was dumbfounded when I read this paper."

Fine, I thought. You try being me and writing it.

"I need to tell you something. Or inform you."

I'd taken the scenic route again.

"I'll be using it in future classes as an example of a successful execution of this assignment."

"My grade?" I asked.

"Highest possible," he said. "Obviously."

Nothing obvious about it, I thought. Gold afternoon sun flickered though the slitlike window onto the edge of his wire-rim glasses. I shook my head. "Are you ill?" he asked me. He shoved a wastebasket in front of me. I moved my chair so light wouldn't hit his glasses, so the tiny star on the corner of the lens would stop pulsing. I started to cry.

I hadn't cried since my sister was in the hospital, chattering like a baby. That was sad too. I cried from relief. The paper would make or break me; I'd been made. I cried because I'd worked while Kristine watched with a hurt expression because she knew something was wrong and I didn't confide, and she was too mistaken about my character to assume the worst, that I was doing drugs at work; I didn't do phone calls at work. I'd hurried to meet Dr. Stoat, who thought I was good, but I almost wasn't. Then I remembered Vanzetti, who looked

more stricken, more woebegone than Sacco, less ready for the end to
which his pamphlets and faith in righteous objection to unjust authority had led.

I needed to make a quick exit from Dr. Stoat's office.

He hadn't pictured his future at a small state college. He'd likely
read a memo from Student Medical Services about suicide preven-
tion—a kind word here or there making a difference. Separate facili-
ties for mental health didn't exist, so he couldn't send me there. He
said, "Are you failing other classes?" I'd have my best GPA so far. I said
so. He produced a crisp, white handkerchief and gave it to me. I de-
murred: how would I get it back to him? He waved his hand in the air,
impatient. "You're in trouble. Am I right?"

I must have nodded.

He said, "You're not the first female college student to find herself
pregnant."

I stopped crying. I was deciding how to say I was in a different trouble, drug-related. But not that. His glasses were dull now, unlit. *Spiral
of silence*, I thought. It hove into view. *Those with an opinion in the minority don't speak.* We were two people in a room. I wasn't a minority.
Yet I was minor. He was major. He waited for me to answer.

When I got home, I hauled my bike into the parlor and leaned it against
the piano. I took a bath. Wearing a robe, my hair in a towel, I used the
green phone in the hallway to call James. I wanted to yell at him for giving me LSD. But I'd pretended I'd had it before. I wanted to yell at him
for sleeping through the bad part while I'd gone home, cut out newspaper photos, decorated and undecorated the bathroom, then worked.
"It was busy," I said at last. I described the streaks of light behind moving silverware. He said, "They call those trails." What was *High Times*
for if not to hone your vocabulary? I told him about riding my bike, but
not that I'd felt I was pedaling in place like the witch in the tornado.
"I got an A on my paper," I said. He said, "You went to campus today?
Man, I slept."

The weight we'd thrown around shifted. I didn't care anymore if he liked my coat or, come summer, my homemade sundresses that looked winsome and breezy with matching flip-flops, two for a dollar at Woolworth's. LSD is best taken in glorious weather when you aren't jostling for power with your boyfriend, I decided. That summer, we made love outside, fireflies flashing. Or the moon shone, and we swam near a waterfall someone made by attaching corrugated tin to posts and stretching it across a creek. I fumbled upward in the downstream until my hands grasped the tin's edge: all that roiling and churning demystified. I had a solid A going in Shakespeare II, another in Spenser class, both taught by a professor I'd been warned would be hardest. Yet every unfamiliar idea was footnoted, and every progress was a story: rise, fall, rise. "Ah, but you have a knack for getting past the literal to layers of symbols," Dr. D. Douglas Waters said.

I met stolid, marriageable boys—in class, at Sigma Tau Delta meetings. But at a small college people know you by reputation. Jimi Hendrix, *Are You Experienced*? Yes. I'd had that interlude with a thirty-two-year-old factory worker. I dated a drug dealer. I wore odd clothes. But Bob Barr's bungled compliment had taught me that you can break one rule if you imbed the broken rule in the midst of convention. I'd wear jeans, a black leotard, then add just my coral-colored jacket with silver-embroidered poinsettia flowers—one of two pieces from an old lady sleeveless-dress-with-matching-jacket ensemble. Then, for a poetry event, I'd wear just the sleeveless dress with plain black tights.

A girl from Oconomowoc—a wealthy Milwaukee suburb, James told me—dated one of James's roommates, and she asked me to live with her and two of her friends next year.

But before the lease began, I did LSD one more time, and James promised to stay awake. He didn't. I shook him gently, and he started yelling, and maybe he couldn't stop because he remembered none of this later, but he shoved me out his bedroom door, toward the stairs, telling me to go, go. He didn't throw me. Or did. Who can say now? I tumbled down, one bruising step at a time, and walked home in the dark in my pink negligee, circa 1959. When he phoned the next day to say where had I gone and thank God I was okay, I broke up with him.

But the next time I worked, Bob Barr dropped off James in the parking lot across from the café. Kristine stared out the window. "Were you expecting him?" she asked. She could tell by my face I wasn't. She said the dishwasher would walk me to my car. I shook my head no. I drove James home and said not to embarrass me at work. A few days later I came out of class, and he was waiting.

Dogged pursuit of an aloof woman is celebrated in Renaissance poems. The woman's refusal will whet the lover's desire—even if this isn't what you want. Next, James broke his leg because he went skydiving, perhaps to demonstrate vigor and biological fitness. Why now? I thought. Finals were starting. He was failing Social Work 3305, Human Behavior and Social Environments. I had an exam the next day, but I brought him food. A week later, Bob Barr called me on the green phone and said that James—who'd used Bob Barr's car to get his license, then bought himself a car, then rolled it while driving fast, possibly drunk—wasn't injured, except his leg was still broken.

"He needs you," Bob Barr said. "He's bad off."

I felt responsible. Intro to Psychology talk about "boundaries" hadn't begun yet.

I made a deal with James. I'd be his girlfriend if I didn't have to see him often. We'd have sex, but not over and over. One orgasm for each of us each time. "I have less spare time than you," I said. I couldn't stop him from doing drugs. He sold a few kinds, all of which I'd sampled, then, curiosity sated, I got back to work. But I didn't want them now.

I moved with the girl from wealthy Oconomowoc and her two friends into a cream-colored house. My mother visited. Someone mentioned James. My mother said: "Who?" He had trouble sticking to my schedule, so he'd drop by, wearing aftershave, and leave pot in a box my roommates kept on the table. He conversed about blues guitar with one roommate, social work with another. The girl who'd invited me to live there loved cocaine. We'd start to wash dishes, scrub the bathroom. She'd say: "Call James and get some coke over here, so we can get this place spiffy." She'd do lines with him, then fire up the vacuum, shouting: "Now this is housekeeping. This must be how my grandma felt when she got her first electric washer." But we didn't tell my mother that. "Who is James?" my mother asked again. The coke-roommate said: "Debra's boyfriend."

My mother asked to meet him. I didn't want to give James false hope by introducing him to my mother. I was removing myself slowly, peeling away so he wouldn't notice. But I couldn't describe to my mother James's status as half-boyfriend. I called him.

He answered his door, holding a corsage. He was taking us to dinner, he said. She'd pay, she answered, firm. Then three grubby brothers pulled up, and one handed James money. I hurried my mother back to her car. She said: "Are you kids dealers?" How would a person who didn't sell drugs or date someone who did respond? Flabbergasted, I decided. Flabbergasted, I said, "No, why?" She said, "That boy gave James money." I scrambled. What was wholesome yet enterprising? "James runs a lawn-mowing service," I said. "He sets up accounts and hires people." She wasn't done yet; she was a bookkeeper: "Why was the employee paying the boss?" I stopped working on my facial expression. My mother had been privy to my subterfuges since I was little. "Customers pay the guy, and he brings a percentage to James," I said. She sighed. She weathered bad facts this way: accepting the semblance of a reasonable lie.

I gave notice at the café—Kristine barely spoke as I finished my two weeks—and started at an expensive new restaurant, for better tips. I kept track of James, his schedule. I got cagey about my own. Peter, a boy I knew from Sigma Tau Delta, said to me in a bar, "You don't like intelligent men." Men? I thought. I said, "James is intelligent." Peter said, "You're too insecure to sleep with me." I wasn't. "Prove it," Peter said. I went to his apartment in one of those business districts with a one-room grocery, butcher, tailor, a strip of stores in the old Polish neighborhood, and Peter's room an empty storefront with curtains covering the window, his bed pushed so near we heard chattering pedestrians on the sidewalk. We didn't undress. We talked about Theodore Roethke.

Next, I lived in a blue-collar neighborhood between the tire factory and brewery, in an apartment I shared with a girl doing practice teaching at a nearby school. A man with a PhD doing postdoc research in rivers asked me out. He'd first seen me at James's. When he came to pick me up, he offered me coke. I declined. He said, "I thought you were a coke whore. I couldn't find another reason for a girl like you being over there." My face felt like a mask. I'd seemed like a whore? He'd insulted James too. I said, "This isn't charming date conversation." The PhD said, "He has good drugs, but he's a blowhard. What's with the guitars?" I said, "He plays well." He played well with records. He didn't play with people. He'd never had people, just customers—not counting me, and his mother, who'd called the police to arrest him for breaking curfew after she passed out. "He's had a hard life," I said. "He has ten times more courage than you."

"Whoa," the PhD said. "I didn't know you loved him."

After the expensive restaurant went bankrupt, I took a job at a bar and moved alone to a tiny half-duplex, charming in the summer once I'd redecorated with knickknacks and lace curtains from the thrift store. But winter blew in. The kitchen used to be a porch. The apartment turned cold. I hung a blanket over the kitchen doorway and, in the morning, I found ice-covered dishes in the sink. I wore mittens to make coffee and never covered the kitchen doorway again. I was wrapped in blankets, circling ads for new apartments, when my mother phoned to say that she was buying me a ticket to fly on a prop jet to a hospital in North Dakota because my taskmaster grandmother had terminal cancer.

"You're never home," my mother said. "I call and call and call."

I told her I'd been at class, at work, or studying. Some nights I studied until dawn in the oldest building, Schofield Hall, which stayed open all night. It used to be a laboratory school with secret balconies so normal school professors could observe teaching and learning—ghosts of professors circling as I studied. I didn't tell my mother that on coldest nights I went to James. We had sex. Then he got up to drink as I slept in a warm bed.

She said, "Just to let you know, I don't know where your father is."

She should move on, I said, make a new life. But in a small town filled with bars and strip joints, they'd been not just husband and wife but partners in get-up-and-go. Everything they said, did, wore, drove, established that they weren't lowlifes. She said, "Divorce is impossible. I'd rather be a widow." I was shocked. "You wish he was dead?"

She said, "Did I say that? No."

She needed a plan. I didn't have one.

When I got to the hospital in North Dakota, my sister was already there, holding her new baby. I sat next to my grandmother's bed and studied my niece, her tiny face blinking at light, at motion. At the end of life, my grandmother was docile, benevolent. In the middle of life, my mother was staggered by double losses looming. I saw it in her wilted posture.

When I got home a few days later, it was December.

I was graduating in a few weeks. My grades were As, except Cs in required sections of Physical Education I'd procrastinated until the end: a C in Relaxation because I fell asleep instead of relaxing; a C in Beginning Swimming. The teacher had noticed me the first day, floating easefully, and stared at my face: "There'd better not be anyone in here who already knows how or that's an automatic F." So I feigned helplessness in deep water.

I'd feigned confidence everywhere else.

I'd feigned for roommates, Lana and Maribel.

I'd feigned I was popular enough for the girls in the cream-colored house where once, at a party, when I was dancing to the Rolling Stones, I heard a guy, too well-off for me, ask: "Who's the girl with frizzy hair who digs electronic music?" It seemed like a line from a movie. When I realized he was talking about me I danced like life was a movie. I danced faster, thinking I could measure life out, not in coffee spoons, like J. Alfred Prufrock, that neurasthenic who just needed a job and a few deadlines, but according to the places I'd lived, the parts I'd been forced to play, changing myself as various settings required.

And I'd feigned for Dr. Darden Stoat who, hurrying to get this sticky moment of college teaching behind him, had added, "I hope this predicament won't keep you from finishing your degree. When a problem presents itself, we have options, but options can shrink."

He was saying, for instance, that I could have handled writer's block many ways, but I'd waited too long and had one option, writing my paper in a grueling vigil. He was saying a pregnant college girl could have a baby—back then a college girl who kept her baby married the father, if he could be persuaded. Or she could put the baby up for adoption, dropping out for a semester. Or she'd have an abortion. Maribel, my lovelorn roommate, had an abortion, her parents never the wiser. This was a small school, a small department, and I wasn't dropping out, nor would I hurry to class with a gold ring, swollen with child. I should have told him I wasn't pregnant. But I didn't contradict my elders. For the first time since I'd swallowed tissue paper with a butterfly wing on it the night before, I spoke from deep inside the truths I had available. I said, "This is a nice handkerchief."

For the next three years, I'd be better dressed—at a visiting scholar event, or smiling as I rushed out of class, happy to have received an A—and I'd see Dr. Darden Stoat in the shadows, his human, intimate smile. I'd change my expression. I'd never been pregnant, of course, but I hadn't known where I fit. I'd belonged somewhere, then didn't. I'd been pregnant with hope, that's all. I couldn't begin to explain I wasn't a diamond in the rough with morbid regrets. I'd never been her and was already more.

I graduated and got a job at a cable channel that flashed news on the TV screen. Monday through Friday, the graveyard shift, I took stories off the wire and condensed them. I met a man who seemed wholesome, or his family did. It was time now, I felt: marriage. People my age married. Besides, when I'd get in from work, I'd find my mother in her car in my driveway—who knows how long she'd sat there—saying she had no husband, no children, nothing. I'd take her inside and pour her a drink, though it was morning.

One day my fiancé—he wasn't perfect, but I was good with raw materials, I felt—didn't see any reason to stop using the dealer with the best pot, the best prices. I waited in the car as he went into James's apartment near a school for criminally troubled boys; James worked there, I knew. He was troubled, but not as troubled as the boys, and they responded. Yet he was a drug dealer, I thought, fuming, waiting for my fiancé so we could head off into a life in which I'd get a master's degree in a warmer state, and my fiancé would learn to be employed. He'd come to college on full scholarship but never finished and clerked at stores and played in bands. He was still inside—getting high by now.

Then I looked up and saw James in stocking feet in the snow, knocking on my window. I rolled it down. For a while, we'd been alike. We'd been squared: strengths multiplying, weaknesses multiplying. He was still who we were when we'd met—outsiders in unfamiliar terrain. "Congratulations on your upcoming nuptials," he said.

I might have said back: "I wish you a happy life." But I didn't know yet that I wouldn't see him again except dead-but-alive in dreams I'd have for decades. I said, "Thank you." I cranked my window back up. My fiancé came out. I rolled away scot-free.

Drinks Are on
the House

Reader, I married this fiancé. One year later he left me, hauling himself and his guitars away on Halloween, hours before a party I was hosting. We graduate students socialized with fervor—getting too drunk too soon, ignoring social niceties to cement these new friendships, stories of mishaps our creation myth. Standing at the top of stairs that led to my apartment, I watched zombies and ghouls stream past and thought that the idea of this party had probably seemed better to me than to my husband. After all, it wasn't his master's degree. Dressed as Dale Evans in my husband's left-behind cowboy hat, wearing a yellow-sequined square dance skirt with bulls and bullfighters swirling, I put beer in coolers. It would be a buzz kill to announce my separation leading to divorce, I thought. Perhaps not leading to divorce. I wanted him back. He was family, familiar. *Manners keep us from revealing feelings too soon.* I'd read that in an antique etiquette book.

I greeted people by name who didn't wear masks. A fellow student, a woodsy poet, came as himself in a flannel shirt unbuttoned to display a ceramic medallion on a rawhide string. Three male students came as one of our professors, Ryman Stacker. They wore guayabera shirts, striped book bag/man purses you could buy at head shops, and pins that said: ANITA BRYANT IS A FRUIT FLY; OUT OF EL SALVADOR NOW. Ryman Stacker came too, dressed as Woody Guthrie. He said to the three students, "Ha ha. Imitation, man. Sincerest form of flattery, quote, unquote. Charles Caleb Colton." Other young professors came. At a state school with big graduate programs, but located in the middle of Kansas and far from a city, the best chance to mingle with the local elite was drinking.

Professors who attended graduate student parties were young, male, white; professors who didn't attend graduate student parties were old, male, white. They all had wives who'd typed their dissertations and now taught Freshman English for low pay. *Male and female He made them*, I thought, noting that there weren't female professors here, just female students. But professors implied we might one day be more than educated wives.

The professor I'd come to study with, a scholar with a national reputation in rhetoric, knew one female professor at Carnegie Mellon, another at Stanford. But the job market was difficult, he added. And then: "This mixes badly with marriage, you see. Dreams get sacrificed." Not my dreams, I thought. My husband didn't have a career. My plan was to stop after this degree and teach at a two-year college. Another of my professors just let old ideas slip. Once, I worried aloud about a paper. He said, "It's good you're insecure. Otherwise, with your brains and feminine attributes, you'd scare me."

I'd scared myself, enrolling in this traditional but newfangled program where, for two years, I'd study literature but also rhetoric, Old English, history of the English language, history and theory of grammar. Then, when I finished two years of classes, I'd spend another year studying for exams on eighty books and writing a thesis for which I'd conduct primary research because the professor whose reputation I'd banked on felt that the study of rhetoric in America was in its infancy and his students should not only summarize current research but exhume the untapped material waiting for us in archives all over and broadcast new conclusions to the world. Most of my classmates were focusing on creative writing or literature instead, not rhetoric, and they seemed more self-assured.

Maybe they were. Or maybe they pretended. I did.

As I'd dug deeper into debt to train for a career my family had never heard of, I saw that I had to go not just to three-hour classes, but to readings, receptions, and happy hours. As I did, I worked hard at acting smart, and then I'd notice my husband working harder.

Next, he joined a band, which solved the problem of whether he should go to my events. When I went to his gigs, though, I talked to people he was hell-bent on impressing, including other band member's wives, who said I was "unique," which didn't sound like praise. I started staying home, doing homework and housework, homework and housework. Not quite synonyms, I thought, as I dusted woodwork while mulling over the Great Vowel Shift, due to migration, also the emergence of a prestige accent. Yet I worried I wasn't adopting a prestige outlook, so I'd planned this Halloween party.

People were arriving in hordes now. "What are you supposed to be?" a gorilla asked.

A Ryman Stacker look-alike said, "She's a cowboy's girlfriend, in real life too."

When I first met my husband, he'd played in bands people now call alt-country, hippie and hillbilly influences merged. After we moved to Kansas, he played straight-up country. As he'd switched genres, I'd switched personas; I added farmer's daughter dresses to my repertoire.

As I sewed, I thought how, when I was little and watching *Gunsmoke*, I'd been mesmerized not by the calico-and-lace heroines but by saloon girls, their clothes, eyes, lips, thrilling bits of cleavage. I'd studied women carefully because I'd grow up to be one, I'd reasoned then. But now I wondered if my childhood longing for a quality these women had and I didn't meant that I was a latent homosexual, a phrase people were just starting to use. Yet my longing wasn't for sex but impact: making power fall to its knees.

It seemed wrong to give that up to try for the new power—"women's lib"—that most people didn't want women to have anyway. But I couldn't express my doubts well, and all around me people had refined their women's rights arguments: precise words, sarcastic zingers. So I kept my feelings about whether I wanted to be sultry-powerful or brainy-powerful to myself and avoided choosing by trying to be both, which is to say dowdy.

One of my classmates, Betty, walked in wearing a boa. She said, "I hate it when people call you a free spirit if they mean they think you're a whore." Another classmate, Theresa Minster, came as Charlie Chaplin. She was a lesbian. In Kansas, the word still sounded vaguely kinky, though, when Theresa said it, it sounded dignified. She had a friend, a graduate student from another department, who was also a lesbian, and the two of them knew all sixteen lesbians in the county, who'd formed a softball team. They came in wearing their jerseys. Another classmate, Ray, was gay. Gay men sometimes got treated like lepers then because AIDS was misunderstood. So, for Ray, and Ray's partner, who said to call him Ray's Wife, being gay meant being militant. Ray's Wife grabbed my crotch. "It's not as if I'm a man demeaning you," he said, wearing a dog collar and leash.

The apartment was rocking now.

I lived in the country in a not-quite ghost town—above the old general store. Downstairs, in front, a portico that had once sheltered horse-drawn wagons and, later, automobiles, now covered a bench where my landlady Garnett, who sold antiques, not groceries and sundries, sometimes sat with her friends, Opal and Pearl. These names are real. How could I find better? I have nothing but praise for these semiprecious jewels. They treated me like—Garnett's word—kin. The only other big building besides the store was the empty schoolhouse, where I sometimes did the Jane Fonda workout with young farm wives, including Garnett's daughters. Everyone knew everyone because we were isolated. The bridge that once led straight to the college town had washed out years ago.

The first emergency at the Halloween party that night, not counting my husband leaving, was the shaky portico. Upstairs, it was like a balcony without railings that you got to through spare bedrooms. The first spare bedroom contained childhood mementos my mother had shipped when she'd emptied the attic, preparing for the court-ordered sale of property co-owned with my dad. The next spare bedroom had a door leading to the roof.

In mild weather, I sometimes studied out there. Once, my husband and I had lain there, staring at stars while taking peyote. He'd rambled on about his recurring dream that he drove a school bus that flew through the sky. I hated peyote. But mutual interests are the foundation of marriage. As my husband talked, I realized that the only recurring dream I had involved my teeth crumbling. This didn't seem worth describing, so I talked about Death & Dying, which was the unit all teaching assistants were teaching then, using the same textbook, teaching essays, poems, and stories about death, grading fifty freshman papers about death, and I'd never before quite understood that one life is like one sigh entering a whirlwind, that death itself is a blue-gray square, a not-luminous destination.

But I stopped obsessing about Death & Dying because I had classes to attend and teach, papers to write, floors to vacuum, and—tonight— people to herd off the portico roof.

One of the Ryman Stacker look-alikes had noticed my phone ringing, picked it up, and found me. I could barely hear Garnett saying she'd driven by on her way home from Weight Watchers and didn't mind that I was having a party, but please get people off the portico because it wasn't sturdy, in fact seemed to be swaying, and people on it were dancing and drinking and some might fall. I rushed to the spare bedroom, stuck my head through the door, and yelled for people to come in right now. The portico roof was covered with tar paper, mended many times with tar. In Kansas, in October, it's hot outside. In the living room, my imitation Oriental rug, a favorite wedding present, now had tar footprints on it. I bent over it with a rag and nail polish remover, swabbing. But I quit when Ryman Stacker said,

"You'll save yourself some grief if you accept that tar tracks are permanent figures in the carpet, not exactly what Henry James had in mind, ha ha."

I'd worn limp, floor-length white chiffon—my mother-in-law's wedding dress—when I opened the rug, rolled up, wrapped in reams of silver paper, a gift from my sister, my brother, my dad, and his girlfriend. My sister found the rug in the Sears catalog, knowing that I'd live in apartments, that a rug covers other people's stains. I loved the rug and wanted it to stay pristine. I wanted my marriage to stay pristine. But before the wedding my not-yet husband and I had packed up in the northern Wisconsin town where we'd met. We were set to leave for the southern Wisconsin town where his family lived. It was on the way to Kansas. Having the wedding there would help my family use company manners, I felt.

My mother claimed to get ill, or really did, when she was in the same room as my father, who wouldn't come to my wedding, or anyone's, or a christening, without his girlfriend. So my nuclear family, having exploded, came to my wedding. So did my gambling grandfather, a widower. I unwrapped the long tubular package, the rug. I'm not the kind of person to forgo makeup at a ritual occasion photographed for posterity, but I'd gotten pink eye in those baffling days before the wedding, and it spread to both eyes before I saw a doctor. I couldn't wear mascara, and people assumed I'd been crying.

I hadn't cried, but people thought I had because, before my not-yet husband and I headed south for the wedding, someone had knocked at the door. My not-yet husband answered it, waved me away. When he turned around, he held papers. He'd been served. The child was five years old. The child's mother had called my not-yet husband months earlier to say she'd had to tell the state or she wouldn't get food stamps. My not-yet husband hadn't told me because he'd hoped it wasn't true. He'd also worried I'd feel upset. When I found out four days before the wedding, I said the child deserved financial support. I felt upset. I said the child deserved to know his father. I felt upset. I said my not-yet husband had known for months; for five years, he must have had an inkling. I felt upset.

My not-yet husband was a fool, irresponsible. But he hadn't cheated. The child had been conceived back when I was James Stillman's girlfriend. The mother was someone my not-yet husband had met in bars—*groupie* was too harsh a word for a woman who'd liked a local band. What a price to pay for a two-night stand, I thought, though she no doubt loved her child. Would I call off the wedding? The U-Haul, packed to its seams, sat in the street. The church in southern Wisconsin awaited. We'd signed a lease in Kansas. I'd stepped onto, not an escalator, but something flat and moving forward.

My husband and I told his family—father, mother, brothers, sisters—about the paternity suit. We sat in their living room with blond paneling, furniture with wagon-wheel and saddle motifs, and talked about this fact, this new relative, illegitimate, though the word sounded awful. A child doesn't ask to be born. A child is legitimate, I said. My not-yet-mother-in-law asked me if I was feeling okay, her eyes gentle. My not-yet-father-in-law seemed closer to tears than anyone. As everyone watched my face, I said we'd find a way to pay child support. A mistake had been made, but years ago. It was lost on me that a continuous mistake had been made for the last five years running, and it wasn't ours but his. Marriage is for sharing, I thought. Yet we weren't married, not until morning.

We moved to Kansas, and child support payments fell into the pile of monthly bills. Our responsibility beyond that was a knot to be untangled when my husband and I would visit Wisconsin, where he used to play a mix of blues, bluegrass, rock—music that lampooned redneck prejudices, even if rednecks in the audience didn't know it. "Up against the Wall, Redneck Mother." Some rube on a barstool always thought this was an anthem.

My husband used to understand it was denunciation. He smoked pot. He smoked it for breakfast. He had gay friends from when he'd majored in music. He used to have a FREE NELSON MANDELA bumper sticker on his guitar case. After we moved to Kansas, he took it off. I asked why, and he said he was making room for new stickers. But he'd left on other stickers that advertised bars. "You're redecorating your guitar case," I said. I understood, peer pressure. But we were moving in opposite directions. I was enrolled in a class called Patriotism and Pornography in Seminal American Texts, and he'd started laughing at jokes where the punchline was that certain ethnicities are subhuman. I recognized the need for protective veneers, but underneath them you have beliefs, ever-refining.

"You didn't think that joke you laughed at was funny, did you?" I asked one night, as we drove home from a gig. I was unsettled, too, because one of the band wives—they were younger than me—had said I looked good for my age. I was twenty-four.

So I maybe seemed like a stranger to him too. He'd met me while I was working for the news channel. He wasn't used to me agonizing about twenty-page papers, or muttering Wallace Stevens poems while making meatloaf. "So neurotic," he'd say, patting me. I'd been raised to defer to the husband, but also to work hard, tidy up, pay bills. Had I erred on the side of competence? I'd taken over legal matters, finances, laundry, cooking. What else could I do? Garnett, conversing in the store one day, let drop this nugget: "A woman doesn't always have to have an orgasm. Sometimes it's enough to give the man his." I'd been fascinated that a woman almost old enough to be my grandmother would discuss orgasms. And I absorbed all the marriage survival tips I could.

The Halloween party guests were off the portico roof now. They danced in the living room, the spare bedrooms, the dining room I used for an office, the hall to the bedroom, in the bedroom in a dense U-shape around the brass bed my mother had shipped, her wedding present. By now, I thought, the shocks weathered in my first year of marriage, in the now-tainted week of the wedding, were either water under the bridge (forgivable) or spilled milk (indelible). I glanced at the ceiling with its old wallpaper, parchment-like with silver flowers, and wondered what it must have been like to be a storeowner's wife a hundred years ago—hopes, fears, a husband with impenetrable motives.

I let myself remember the afternoon, the argument. The mail had come and, with it, another notice my husband had bounced checks. This was before check carbons. He didn't use the checkbook register. He bought things and didn't say so. I also told him—though it wasn't germane—that he hadn't monitored the oil levels in his car. He'd burned up one secondhand car I'd spent part of a student loan to buy so he could get to gigs. Then I spent more of my student loan to buy another, and it had been down two quarts last week. I'd checked it myself and refilled. He couldn't live this henpecked, he said. He'd run downstairs and slammed the door. "Fine," I'd yelled. I threw objects downstairs, and they bounced. Then he was back, bounding upstairs for his guitars. He was six-foot tall, with dimples. He left again, firing up his car, probably down a quart already.

People were starting to leave the party in drunken bunches. Theresa Minster, derby hat in hand, said: "Which one is your husband? I've never met him." I could have said he was at a gig. He wasn't. He was probably at the pedal steel player's. He'd slept there before when he'd been too drunk to drive. Impulsively, I said, "He's not here. We're fighting." She looked surprised. I'd mentioned him as a normal husband the day before in the office. I hadn't told anyone about money problems. When I'd complained about the burned car, I made it sound like a vexing but ordinary used car problem. She said, "Not to intrude, but if there's anything I can do, let me know." I nodded. "Thank you."

Then the apartment was empty except for me and the woodsy poet. I'd restocked coolers all night, collected empties, checked the portico. I wanted a drink, but there wasn't one left that wasn't dregs, so I decided to break out the dandelion wine I'd made the spring before, using my husband's grandmother's recipe. I'd picked dandelion blossoms (*must pick in morning*, the recipe stipulated), washed them, added boiling water, sugar, and all-important yeast. I let this stand for three weeks, and strained it into bottles.

I'd set them in the spare bedroom, the one with junk, relics. When light from the window sometimes hit the bottles, they glowed yellow. My husband's grandmother had served hers to company in thimble-sized glasses. This was the first time I'd served mine. It was strong. Every time I served it in the future—at a Thanksgiving dinner that went on after store-bought wine was drained, or at an after-the-bars-closed party—it knocked everyone into another zone. The woodsy poet and I drank this incandescent wine and talked.

He'd gotten married in high school when his girlfriend, named Stevia, after her father Steve, was pregnant. "It was the right thing to do. But it hasn't been the easiest marriage," he said. "That isn't the most original line in the world," I answered, taking off my husband's hat. "Next you should say she doesn't understand you." I was getting drunk fast, monologuing. "But I'd believe you," I added. "I don't understand my husband. He doesn't understand me. It's a big mystery with clues and clues and no solution."

The woodsy poet said, "Where is he tonight? Playing?"

"He's out of town." This was true, if I meant the almost-ghost-town. I slipped off my ivory-flowered cowboy boots. Then came the second emergency of the night. I was married. The woodsy poet was. I had scruples. Could I break this one rule just once? I could. I straddled the woodsy poet on the chair and started kissing. My husband would be induced to come back, I thought, kissing. But I was on a much-needed vacation from marriage, tough work, and in the meantime I'd do this inadvertent coupling, huddling, a splurge.

My husband was living at the pedal steel player's. Headed for campus or the laundromat, I'd drive out of my way to see his car. If I called ABC Western Wear, I could ask for the pedal steel player's phone number—the pedal steel player was engaged to the store owner's daughter. But calling ABC Western Wear seemed awkward. I could go to the pedal steel player's house. But who would answer the door? At home, I waited. The weather turned cold. Each room was heated with a gas stove on the floor I lit by pulling a lever, striking a match. I kept doors between rooms open and let costly heat escape so I could hear the phone. I paused the vacuum cleaner to listen. This was before answering machines. Every time I left, I'd return and stare at the phone, its secret life.

Weeknights passed quickly: homework, grading, chores. I didn't mind Sundays. Dusk was bad, but over in an hour. If I went out on Fridays, I could handle Saturdays—then I'd be hungover, absent-minded, as I bought groceries, cleaned, went downstairs to help Garnett. I'd end propped in the brass bed under the quilt my husband's grandmother made.

I went places with people from school, who sometimes asked where my husband was. At a gig, I'd say. Then Theresa invited me to a black-and-white ball at the VFW, which was available for private parties. Betty, who shared an office with Ray, was going—Ray had told her they'd have cases of that champagne in black bottles, Freixenet. When we got there, Betty, in a houndstooth-checked dress, stood with Ray, who had on white slacks, a black shirt. Ray's partner, wearing a black Speedo and a black-and-white feather headpiece, danced with a man in a weight lifter's suit. I wore a flowing black dress I'd made from inexpensive fabric and lace, my ivory-flowered cowboy boots, and my taskmaster grandmother's pearls. Theresa, in black jeans and a turtleneck, looked annoyed. "Really," she said, "no one could be more unalike than gay men and gay women. It's a political accident we associate at all. It's the Kansas version of Fire Island here."

"What's Fire Island?" I asked.

"Like Woodstock," she said, "except gay sex, gay music."

I nodded. Then she starting talking to someone. The softball lesbians had come, wearing rented tuxedos. In the smoky haze, they looked like a waddle of penguins. One of them asked me to dance. "I won't bite," she said. I didn't want to seem prejudiced, so I danced. Then I found Betty, dancing with Ray, and told her to tell Theresa I'd gone home.

I drove my VW bug with the hole in the floor, its dim lights that were brighter than its brights, but not bright. I squinted. I knew this road. The winter before I'd driven it when a blizzard had dumped twenty inches, and the plow came through, but the wind picked up and snow drifted until everything was level, no difference between the ditch and highway, except one side of the highway was rimmed with electrical poles and wires, and I'd used these as guidelines. But that night, I got home, cranked up the bedroom heater. In the morning, I went to brush my hair, but my hairbrush wasn't in my purse. Maybe it fell out in the car? I went downstairs where my car sat alone. Light snow had sifted down in the night. I found my hairbrush under snow in the driveway, my wallet too.

I'd almost lost my wallet, my two forms of ID.

I got in the car and hurried to the pedal steel player's house. I knocked, then waited. I knocked again. The pedal steel player, a stoic man, answered, wearing pajamas bottoms. He nodded. I hadn't brushed my hair yet. "Hello," he said. He went to a door, banged on it: "Get up. Your wife is here." How useful to be country after all, I thought. We'd surprised no one with our heartaches by the number. My husband emerged wearing his light blue, misshapen bathrobe, which I was used to seeing him wear at home, while eating Cheerios and waiting for his Alka-Seltzer to fizz. "Hi there," he said, friendly.

Puzzled, I asked how he got the bathrobe. He'd been back to get clothes while I was in class. "My shirts haven't been ironed since," he said. I was confused. "You didn't take clothes?" I'd have noticed. "A few," he said. "Your hat?" The one I'd worn on Halloween still hung on its hook. He said, "I have a charge account at ABC Western Wear."

He explained he wasn't coming back. "I'm immature." I said I didn't mind. Day by day, though, I had minded. He said, "You're not immature." Yet I'd assumed that goodwill was enough: marriage's starter ingredient. I tried to remember who'd asked whom, who'd proposed. But all I could remember was that I'd gotten a good scholarship, and he'd wanted to move to Kansas, and my mother was coming to stay with me every weekend then. She wasn't herself, trying to get even with my dad by calling a radio station to advertise his car for sale, breaking into his house to unplug the freezer so a cow's worth of steaks had spoiled. He could get a restraining order against you, I'd warned.

My husband turned to look at me. "Besides, I can't stay married to someone who throws a guitar." I must have looked stunned. "The day I left," he said. I'd thrown a Tupperware bowl and the checkbook downstairs. He'd stepped over them when he came back for his guitars. My voice sounded feeble as I said so. "But then you threw my bass guitar." I pointed out that he'd set the acoustic and the electric bass at the top of the stairs, both in cases designed to get loaded on trailers and driven over bumpy roads to honky-tonks, and he'd taken the acoustic guitar and his best boots downstairs and, when he was halfway back up for the bass guitar, I'd slid its heavy case toward him. You could see this as helping, though I hadn't felt helpful as I'd shoved it—upright, hinges on the bottom, handle on top. Just unhappy. "I'm too stingy to throw something expensive," I said.

He yawned. He wanted to go back to sleep, he said.

I stood up. "If we're getting a divorce, we'll have to talk about details."

He patted me. "I'm not going to grow up anytime soon."

As I drove home, I tried not to think about how he'd set me aside. I worried instead about paying bills without the sporadic money he made. I pulled up in front of Garnett's store. Inside, she and Opal and Pearl were unpacking items from an estate sale. Garnett looked at me, then handed me a brush from an enameled vanity set. She'd endured the death of a child, also her husband's dotage, marked by disinhibition, lechery. Once, someone sent her an anonymous letter that said the store needed a coat of paint right away, unless she meant to put the whole community to shame. Garnett had made Magic Marker placards and stuck them in the ground. JUDGE NOT OR YE SHALL BE JUDGED. WHY DO YOU LOOK AT THE MOTE IN YOUR NEIGHBOR'S EYE? When they were weather-beaten, smeared by rain, I'd helped her take them down. I brushed my hair and told her where I'd been.

Pearl said, "My daughter was married to a no-good too."

Opal, shaking her head, "That's not husband material."

Pearl, "Her new boyfriend thinks she's heaven-sent. A man like that is still coming."

Garnett, "When you can't see what's next, assume it's better." She hugged me.

Late that night, I wondered if maybe I deserved this poetic justice, supernatural retribution, because of my reprieve-fling with the woodsy poet—an idea I put to rest when the band wife who'd told me I looked good for my age called from a bar. "I heard it's over," she said. "Good riddance. I wouldn't put up with stepping out. We women wanted to tell you all along, but Eddie said we couldn't. If Eddie did me like that, I'd glue his dick to his leg with Super Glue." I thanked her, hung up, and I worried about Christmas.

Economical option, I'd stay in Kansas. I asked which classmates would stay. None. I flew home and went to my father's newly purchased cottage on a river. His girlfriend, now my stepmother, went to bed early so my dad and I could talk. He showed me his new TV. I admired it. I told him I still had the old one from the summer cottage. He said, "You're hiding in school. You're afraid of getting a real job." I said that I graded three hundred papers per semester. "Not for pay," he said. Yes, I explained, my fellowship. He said, "Like the dole. And you're educating yourself out of the marriage market."

A few days later, I went to see my mother, who'd moved in with a boyfriend. On the phone, she'd told me he owned a mired-in-debt supper club, and she was taking him and his supper club in hand. When I got there, she was in its kitchen, prep-cooking. The boyfriend sat at the bar and gave me quarters for the jukebox. He liked the song I picked out, "Time after Time," which was sung by the Vienna Boys Choir, he said. I mentioned that it was sung by Cyndi Lauper. Then he called me the last dirty word in the English language.

This word has a respectable history, having appeared as recently as the fourteenth century in its Early Modern English form as a gynecological term—"queynte," in the Wife of Bath's Prologue. It was a medical and private word for another three hundred years, but it wasn't considered lewd until the seventeenth century. I said so the second time he said it, as in: "High-on-your-horse, know-it-all cunt." Good thing

I didn't visit often, my mother said later. He didn't eat well. "What?" I asked. "He's a picky eater, so he doesn't have food in his stomach when he drinks." When I went to bed, he was drinking vodka. When I got up he was, but—concession to dawn—he'd added orange juice.

The supper club was next to his house, so well insulated you couldn't see outside, windows dripping with condensation. My bedroom was in the basement. That night, I woke to noises and shrieks. My mother's boyfriend was overturning furniture. She came down to wake me. We listened to him stomping, smashing. We spent the night with the door locked, though we worried he'd knock it down. My mother sat on the floor. "You have no idea how hard marriage is." Maybe I didn't. Maybe my one-year marriage didn't count. I said, "But you're not married. Leave him." She couldn't. She'd put her savings into his business. I wondered how long she'd known him when she did. Yet I'd spent a student loan on my shirker husband. She said, "I'll have to marry him to get it back."

Did I understand that being a middle-aged divorcée in a small, frozen town had made her feel redundant, a reverse spinster, without even a widow's status, so she'd taken the first man on offer? Yes. Did I worry she wasn't safe? Yes. Did I know that her situation would cast a shadow over her life and mine for years to come? No. I was young, a sad-circumstances-that-can't-be-averted novice. I saw her life as a problem I'd solve by phone once I got home, a plan that would turn out to be unworkable, but I didn't know that yet either. And I had to survive this visit, which was going badly, she intimated, because her kids, evidence of her previous, solvent, reputable life, made him insecure.

Then the fee-fie-fo-fum stopped. He'd passed out. Christmas Day went on as usual: gifts, food, the radio playing carols. My mother's boyfriend got up at noon, jaunty. Relieved, my mother asked him to drive me to the airport at three a.m. the next morning for my seven a.m. flight. We were barreling down the road, the temperature at minus thirty, when the car heater broke. We went to a gas station, found a piece of cardboard to put in front of the grill to keep air from blowing through the grill as wind-chilled air as opposed to merely unheated air. But because we'd hunted for cardboard at gas stations predawn, I missed my flight. Chagrined, my mother's boyfriend paid for my changed ticket. I flew to Kansas. I drove three hours in whirling snow to the almost-ghost-town.

Neither maid nor matron, who was I? In Garnett's store, I found a book of old movie stills. I was Greta Garbo, I decided. I bought a carton of cigarettes, an antique ashtray, an art deco lighter that looked good in my apartment. I forced myself to smoke no less than four cigarettes a day, never skipping even that first bad one with coffee, but I never got past the nausea unless I was drinking. I cut my hair so it fell across one eye. I spent the last of a student loan to buy retro sweaters, fuzzy, feminine, that I wore with trousers.

Country music, inescapable in Kansas, wasn't my druthers. Every morning I listened to jazz, torch songs, until it was time to get dressed for class. Then I'd stop brooding and put on my makeup. I loved classes I was taking. I loved teaching, students entrusting to me their faith in self-improvement, then coming back to report that they'd started getting higher grades in every class. One day, I told my students what pitfalls to avoid as they took on a new, more demanding paper. I said, "See you next class period." I felt euphoric. I wondered—as I did every morning when I woke—what I'd been sad about before I'd been unconscious. Then I'd remember, oh that: my husband found me dispensable.

Max found me in a graduate student bar. He wasn't a student. His money came from cocaine, which he'd offer me, and I'd decline. He owned a huge house surrounded by piles of firewood. Its windows were covered with light-blocking, thermal blinds that tacked down with wing-nuts and metal eyelets. He thought fossil fuels would run out in the next decade. I didn't see a future with this libertarian with a penchant for dystopian novels and a conviction that Western civilization was on the brink of ruin. Yet, despite his depend-on-no-one view, he'd cook for me, buy me wine. We'd have sex for hours, good for relaxation. He didn't believe in monogamy, but he hadn't expected to like me. For me, he said, he'd give monogamy a whirl. Yet I couldn't be around more than one night a week, school work. Plus, I needed money—I'd taken a job at a bar by the gravel pit.

When I walked in for my first Saturday afternoon shift, customers in sweaty T-shirts and feed caps went silent. The owner, showing me the ropes, said: "Yes, we have a heifer on the premises. At ease, gentlemen." I felt unsafe. A customer who wasn't a regular said, "When do you get off work, little lady?" Asa, who wore a cowboy hat and sat at the bar, told him: "Best mind your manners." Another regular, a pig farmer, grabbed the new guy and made a fist. Asa told the pig farmer to calm down. He told the new guy to find another bar. When spring arrived—redbud blooming against the prairie, temporarily green now—Asa and I went catfishing. Or we'd ride in his jacked-up pickup.

The sun set, red. Or stars glittered. With the windows rolled down, we'd ride over hills, down into valleys, lush pockets of cold air, crickets chirping. Once, we parked by the river. When Asa leaned over for a kiss, his hat slid off. I'd been around Kansas long enough to know that men who never take off their hats are bald. Asa was really bald—this makes any man look low-browed, exposed. Moonlight flickering through the bug-spattered windshield turned his head mottled, unearthly. I said I wanted to have sex. He put his hat back on and said, "I don't think so. You say you do. But you seem gun shy."

Max had pointed out that he wasn't mean. He said he loved me. "You're my best girl," he added. But pretending to be someone he wasn't, someone who didn't sleep with other women when I was too busy, wasn't feasible, he said. So I stopped seeing him, though sometimes, home alone at two a.m. and wondering what high standards were for if no one knew I had them, I'd call Max, and he'd answer, at first sleepy, then his voice turned seductive in a too-practiced way, or that's how he sounded aroused, and he'd drive fast to my apartment. Some high-level pining had been set off in me, an alarm. When Billie Holiday sang about a Lover Man, where was he, at first I thought she meant he was across town with someone else. It took me a while to understand Lover Man didn't exist.

I thought about Betty from school, who pined for someone who wouldn't make their nighttime affair a daytime affair, and she was pined after by the woodsy poet, who'd hardly been with anyone but his high school girlfriend, now his wife. "Maybe it's that Betty's out of reach," the woodsy poet said one day. The man Betty wanted was out of reach. The economy of love, I thought. One person wants someone more than the other one does, and the one who wants most has least power. Because Max hedged his bets with spare lovers, he had power. If he wanted me more, I wouldn't want him. Not Asa either. Not my husband, who once offered to do the leg work to get our divorce because he felt bad he'd done so little when we were married. But months passed. "You file," he said.

I found a lawyer, money for the lawyer, started proceedings. I was in the last year of my degree, reading for comprehensive exams, doing research for my hundred-page thesis. But I couldn't write it. I consulted books about writer's block. The consensus seemed to be that you distract yourself, write casually, carefree, until you feel excited. I stayed unexcited. I dithered away months, a semester, taking a "Progress" instead of a "Credit" for my thesis grade. And I celebrated Halloween that year by going to bars that teemed with costumed students. I wore a mauve suit, circa 1940, I'd found at a thrift store, also a hat with a veil I got at Garnett's store; I clipped a fountain pen to a notepad. Dressed as a stenographer—a menstruating stenographer, I thought—I popped Midol and drank.

Then it was a Saturday in December. Theresa Minster came to my apartment to cook chicken parmesan. She'd worked as a butcher, and she'd brought her own knives. She sliced expertly, next to the bone, as she talked about Asa, "the bald guy from the gravel pit," she said, not quite accurately, and Max, "bad news," she said, "amusing, yes, because I've yakked with him in the bar too, but a sociopath." We talked about Betty, where she'd go next year, because she'd applied to a PhD program based on where the man she loved had applied. After he broke up with her, she'd torn up a letter from the school.

Theresa and I zipped through a bottle of store-bought wine, then got out the dandelion wine. Theresa said we should put on coats and sit on the roof. "It's safe for two people, right?" she asked, remembering the Halloween party. It was. I watched sunsets out there. Dawn. Wind making the tall wheat rise, fall, and roll like waves. Tonight the sky was pocked with stars. Theresa and I sat, backs to the wall, and I said that Betty's letter was likely neither an acceptance nor rejection, just information, because it was early. Graduating at last, I'd applied to PhD programs and was waiting to hear.

If I moved, I thought, I wouldn't be able to afford an apartment this big. When I worked at the store, Garnett paid me in credit, and my rooms had become a shrine to someone else's domestic history. I had a Shirley Temple milk pitcher; ceramic statues of dogs, remnants from a 1920s collecting craze; mirrors with hand-painted borders; a plaque made mosaic-style from crushed, colored tinfoil that read GOD BLESS THIS HOME COOKING.

Theresa said, "You can't keep splitting time between Max and Asa."

I thought about my soon-to-be-ex-husband, how I'd married his faux-bucolic ideals and soundtrack to match. Or I'd fallen in love with his family. I'd put up preserves, cooked, cleaned, ironed. What did I take from this insight? Don't marry a facade.

Theresa said, "You're at a crossroads."

I'd temporarily lost my goal, yes. Teaching at a two-year college had suddenly seemed wrong. I'd be an old maid schoolmarm, no husband, children, nothing. But I was in too deep. I'd requested documents from archives at universities across the country, sorted them into tidy but guilt-inducing piles around my apartment. Dreams get sacrificed, I'd think, not writing. I made charts, outlines. I refined my title, "Fact and Fiction: The Artificiality of the Distinction between Expository and Creative Writing." The genres became separate in the twentieth century, I'd argue, because of the history of the American English department. I got down to the wire, eight weeks, still nothing. I worried in front of Asa, whose advice was to stop saying that I couldn't go on, forward. I asked Max for pot. I wrote my thesis stoned, spattering my-self and my desk with Wite-Out.

My acclaimed advisor had beamed. "By God, this is publishable. Essentialist preconceptions revealed as historical fluke. This should be a monograph." What's a monograph? I'd wondered. The other pro-fessors praised my research, my peculiar organization they charitably described as a rejection of rigid genre definitions. Three weeks before my qualifying exams—covering forty books of literature, forty books of rhetoric—I stopped smoking pot, which overcame inhibitions, I knew, but hurt short-term memory.

Theresa said, "I mean that neither Max nor Asa share your inter-ests."

Combined, they almost did. Asa suited the part of me raised to be a farm wife. Max was so considerate in bed and inconsiderate ev-erywhere else I'd forget I'd hoped to be a scholar. I didn't date class-mates—dating would seem like homework. The distance between my aspiring daytime self and my nighttime self had widened. I said, "You mean I should date someone like Shawn?" Shawn was one of the stu-dents who'd come to last year's Halloween party dressed like Ryman Stacker, not that Shawn was interested in me, a cowboy's castoff who dressed like Greta Garbo now. With my marriage done for and wrap-ping up, I felt older than Shawn. Did that work? I'd never wanted to be the man's elder.

Theresa threw her hands in the air. "Why? Are you attracted to him?"

I said, "He's nice."

Theresa sighed. "I always fall for straight women. You couldn't tell?"

I felt guilty. But so far I hadn't worried that Theresa might be inter-ested in me, because if I had I'd have participated in what she'd called homophobia, a new word to me then: the bigoted tendency to assume that gay people were trying to turn everyone gay.

"Yes, I did say that," she agreed, slumped.

I started to put my arm across her shoulder. Then stopped. I'd once kissed my college roommate, the girl from wealthy Oconomowoc. We'd been in a bar, and boys were hitting on us, and my roommate from Oconomowoc flew into a rage and yelled, "Enough. We're lesbians. Leave us alone." The drunk boys yelled: prove it, prove it. Drunk ourselves, my roommate and I kissed, a slow and histrionic kiss. It had the wrong effect. The boys cheered loud, lusty. So we paid for our drinks and went to a different bar.

But when I'd pretend-kissed my roommate from Oconomowoc, it was in the middle of a conversation about how she wanted her old boyfriend back, a not-pretend kiss from a prince of a guy. This was different. I turned to Theresa in the dark. Did I feel recoil? I'll never know. I felt recoil for considering recoil. I didn't want to recoil from a lesbian who was my friend. "I like you," I said. This wasn't a wide-eyed prick-tease line, like: I care for you but not that way. I meant I was heterosexual. Or, if I believed recent talk that sexuality is fluid, sexual identification cultural, then I was conventional; I'd been raised, cultivated like a crop, to settle on a man. So had Theresa—her parents were well meaning yet baffled, she'd said. But Theresa likely had different genetic markers than me, though the science that would suggest this hadn't been developed yet. I said, "Let's call it a night. You sleep on the couch. You better not drive."

I got her a pillow and blankets. I kissed her goodnight. How long? *Did you kiss Mrs. Tilton?* Henry Ward Beecher had been asked this during his adultery trial. He was the country's first celebrity preacher, and people are prurient. *A holy kiss as I have sometimes seen it in poetry.* I'd read the transcript in an American Studies class. That night, I kissed Theresa too long. I meant that I felt friendly, open-minded, not sexual. This is a lot to convey by kissing. I smoothed over a rough situation, not realizing that removing hope is like removing Band-Aids, best done fast, no frills, sympathy dispensed later.

In the morning, I wore my chenille robe as we hugged goodbye in the doorway. Garnett passed us on her way to church and either thought I was dating a slender young man or that a woman had visited me early, maybe dropping off homework, hugging over homework.

On Monday, I saw Ryman Stacker on campus, and he asked about my plans. I told him that I'd meant to quit after this degree and let my husband explore options, but we'd split up. His band had split up. The best musicians—the ones who didn't get drunk on stage—were moving to Nashville. "Maybe I'll get a PhD. There's no one around to mind."

Ryman Stacker said, "Ha ha. Decisions and revisions, T. S. Eliot."

That afternoon, sitting in my kitchen, I contemplated my first solitary Christmas.

The black phone shivered and rang. The possibilities weren't infinite: Asa, Max.

I answered. "Hello?"

Theresa cleared her throat. "I want to say in my defense that there are more straight women than gay women in the world. That was a hard mistake to avoid." I sighed. I understand mistakes, I thought. She said, "There's a time for candor, and a time to keep ideas to yourself. It must have been your dandelion wine, truth elixir." I wasn't listening carefully now because a florist's van was pulling into my driveway, looking for directions to somewhere else. But, no, the driver got out, holding cellophane-wrapped flowers, consulting his clipboard, my mailbox: 229B. Now he was knocking. "My gosh," I said, hopeful and ingenue-like in spite of myself. "Someone has sent me flowers."

Theresa said, "You're kidding."

Lover Man, I thought. A one-size-fits-all for my variegated selves, someone I knew but hadn't noticed yet, announcing his arrival. I left Theresa on the phone as I rushed downstairs, signed for the flowers, hurried back, ripped open the card. "Thinking about you at Christmas. Love, Dot." My not-yet-ex-mother-in-law. Last clue. Mystery over.

A copper-colored kettle with red mums and sprigs of evergreen. On the phone, Theresa said, "From the bald cowboy?" I said, "Not even. They're from my former husband's mother." Theresa started laughing. "I'm sorry I'm laughing," she said. And I thought about how my old professor Dr. D. Douglas Waters once said in class that the difference between who we are and who we hope to be is a chasm. Yes.

We live there, suspended, pulled one way and another. I looked at the mums, the attached fake-gold sleigh bauble. Theresa said, "Agree with me. This is funny." She seemed too amused. Maybe she had a right. She understood me better than I did yet. Did I owe her? I said, "Funny."

Let me pause now, intermission, and say that people disappear.

Consider this moment, years in the future, when I had a professional job, but I wasn't tenured yet, not permanent, and my mother
had married her heart-attack-waiting-to-happen boyfriend, who'd
died. I told my recently promoted department chair—once the hiring committee chair who'd said she admired we daring young women
coming straight through with our PhDs—that I needed a few days off
for a family funeral. This isn't some waitressing job, I reminded myself. At a grown-up job you get bereavement leave. The department
chair lifted her pen and said, "Let me express my condolences. Please
excuse me for asking, but I need to know who's died." I said, "My stepfather. I want to go to the funeral for my mother's sake. This counts as
bereavement, I hope?" I left out that my mother and I were—to use the
shorthand—estranged, though we'd never argued. After years of little
to no contact, I didn't know my mother. She didn't know me.

My department chair said, "Well, the changing shape of family. You
must go."

Hard on the land wears the strong sea and empty grows every bed.

I've never lived near the sea. The social net grows thin, I thought, picturing the social net as one of those frayed curler caps my wandering grandmother used to wear to breakfast.

In stories, people don't disappear. Every character who mattered just a little makes an appearance, another appearance, another. In the last chapter, everyone who's weighed in on page 1, page 81, page 181, reappears. Or news of them does. In life, though, people vanish. Remembering what someone said to me on a tar-covered rooftop in Kansas—or in green fields flecked with yellow, or cheap rented rooms, or a house in Colorado, a professor's office, a café with an odd menu—is historic preservation. I moved on; people I knew didn't or went somewhere else. Most never met each other. Expecting them to recur and attend a crowded, friendly finale is to expect an old-fashioned story with coincidences and mirage-like continuity, a fable.

The chorus, too, should be regarded as one of the characters.

For centuries, people left farms for cities. Before that, their ancestors left old countries for new countries. People roam. Sometimes they settle down. Once, a sixth cousin addicted to genealogical research ("recovery is not an option!"), contacted my father, my sister, my brother, me. She said my wandering grandmother didn't speak proper German but Plattdeutsch and lots of Yiddish. My father didn't believe it, even when I showed him a Yiddish dictionary and he recognized words. This distant cousin on my dad's side contacted my mother too, since she'd procreated with my dad. My mother resented this recording of birth, death, marriage. Our twig on the family tree was messy.

In small towns, divorce won't help you move up the social ladder with its miniscule rungs magnified by gossip. My parents hated their divorce. They hated mine. My sister, fully recovered from her accident, had a burst of clarity, realizing she had just one life. She shocked everyone by getting divorced too, going new places, wearing new clothes. "Like Debra," my father said, appalled. She remarried. My parents sighed, relief.

Before my parents' divorce was final—the property sold and divided—my father lived with my stepmother in what I thought of as the ancestral home, though we'd lived there for just my childhood. My stepmother walked on carpets my mother had selected (too gaudy, my stepmother felt), pulled shut at night drapes my mother had saved to buy (so old-fashioned, my stepmother said). I didn't like hearing my mother's taste criticized, but my stepmother was trying to be herself, get acquainted. *The reasons for reciprocity in self-disclosure will hove into view.* A few years later, she had the wild idea to fly to Kansas without my father, to visit me. Yes, I said. I'd passed my qualifying exams. I'd dropped off my thesis with a typist who'd bought one of those new computers that word-processed, and I felt momentarily so free. I never did figure out my stepmother's age. She looked younger than my father but like a bobbysoxer, not a post-hippie. She'd had a rough girl-hood, I gathered, no time for parties. When she got to Kansas, I took her to parties.

I introduced her to classmates as my stepmother. "Wicked step-mother," she said, giggling. We visited Max, and she asked to see pot. She didn't want to smoke it, just see it. He got out the tray he kept in his pantry and rolled a joint as she watched. The next day, my stepmother and I wandered through stores, and she surprised me again by buying herself a camisole and panties with Minnie Mouse motifs. I tried on a copper-colored, satin blazer marked down from $165 to $35, quick clearance, then put it back. "You can't afford $35?" she said, skeptical. I was down to bare bones, waiting to find out my future. No new clothes just now; I said so. She said, "But what would you wear it with anyway?"

I said, "A black top, faded jeans, my high-heeled boots." A few min-utes later she bought it. "Why?" I asked. It didn't seem like her. Or, with her teased, bouffant hair, she'd look like Tammy Wynette in it. Where in Spooner would she go dressed like that? She said, "Well, it was good enough for you. You think I can't pull it off then?" I didn't say anything else because she seemed upset, and I was still thinking it was weird she liked Minnie Mouse underwear. Then, when I'd driven her to the airport and walked her to the gate, she pulled the blazer out and shoved it toward me. "Gosh, you're hard to surprise," she said, laugh-ing. But she went home and my dad had drunk too much with the door open, and he passed out over the threshold. She told me this by phone when I asked her to visit again someday. She couldn't; he might have died of hypothermia, she said. We've had moments since, lucky eye contact, unspoken mutual hilarity. But being my dad's wife wore her down, and that carefree stepmother I could have known vanished too.

I cultivated instead short-term affection: high-risk, high-reward. The lie I told myself was that I'd stay in touch. I'll come back to visit, I promised Garnett as we walked through the apartment one last time, now a cavernous set of rooms with mock-limestone paneling made of spongy cardboard, but also that starry wallpaper on the ceiling over a hundred years old. My knickknacks, my doilies, my lace curtains, my imitation Oriental rug with traces of tar, had made it seem welcoming. Garnett didn't see why she was inspecting the apartment before returning my deposit, she said, because I was a good housekeeper. We chatted for a minute about the next renter, a daughter of the man who owned the bar by the gravel pit, how she wouldn't be able to make the place homey. I pictured bean bag chairs, plastic end tables, beer posters. Garnett said, "I don't mind an occasional party, but if it's all the time and a rough crew I'll give her notice." I smiled.

I was Garnett's favorite. Had I ever been anyone else's? We hugged goodbye, and she broke down, tears streaking her face dusty with lavender-scented powder. She took off her glasses, which caught in her hair, her topknot, which tumbled down, dark, undulant.

I wrote to her, and she wrote back. The last time was after my thesis advisor sent me a newspaper clipping—he took pride in students he'd launched, and he knew I'd lived in the almost-ghost-town. It said that Garnett's youngest son had been smothered while driving a backhoe in the gravel pit when gravel mounds toppled. I wrote to Garnett. She answered: "Thank you and know that I love you, but don't worry about me. And maybe it's good Tim can't feel the shame his father has heaped down upon us." Her husband, a randy old man whom even Garnett avoided, had run off with a barfly. I hadn't lived long enough to know what to say back. My news was trivial, plans coming together, not apart. I never heard from Garnett again, though, as I write this, having run her name through an Internet search engine, she's alive, a survivor in her eighty-six-year-old brother's recent obituary.

I found an 1880s photo of the store too, a general store. According to the website, the upstairs rooms where I lived once served as a courthouse for a county seat long since gone. The land is different, no trees; people in front look like characters in a Mark Twain story.

But the building is the same. I count my windows: one for my kitchen where I answered the phone; one for my dining room where I wrote and studied; one for my living room where I listened to records; one that would become the door to the portico roof, not yet built; one for the spare bedroom where I stored relics my mother shipped when she emptied my childhood home. The apartment was a cheap place to live until I could afford better, yet decades later I wake in my king-size bed, and I find I've dreamed I'm moving back in, and there's a surprise-door leading to space I didn't know existed. The surprise-door is in the spare room, where I'd stashed cargo I cast off when I moved: embroidered dish towels turned ragged; the *My School Years* scrapbook my taskmaster grandmother sent; bottles of dandelion wine I made using husband #1's grandmother's recipe.

That apartment is the second-to-last place I saw my mother for nearly twenty years. I understand now that when I saw her in Kansas our era of telephone-only contact was beginning, but I'd assumed we were just in a short spell when visiting each other was inconvenient.

On the phone with my mother, then, I said I was driving across western Kansas, eastern Colorado, north to Wyoming, west into Utah. I wouldn't throw away my bed, my books, my desk, my sewing machine, the parquet-inlay table with matching chairs, and a few more pieces I'd earned at Garnett's store. I was renting a U-Haul truck, towing my small car. My mother must have worried into a froth in front of her boyfriend, not yet her husband. Or, sober, he wanted to be kindly acquainted. My mother called the next day and said to rent a trailer, not a truck, and the two of them would drive from Wisconsin to Kansas, tow the trailer to Utah, unhitch it, then drive down to Arizona, snowbird haven, to check it out for future business schemes, then drive back to Wisconsin. "We love road trips," she said, a girl in love. I was relieved, grateful. I'd been scared to drive a big rig while towing a car, the last stretch into Salt Lake City so steep, I'd heard, that brakes give out.

I left pots and pans unpacked, and I'd been told to buy specific groceries. My mother's boyfriend ate only a few foods, canned corn, ground round, and on Fridays—he was Catholic—tuna in white sauce over toast. I'd also been told to have everything else packed because there'd be no time to linger, so the apartment looked as unappealing as it did the next day when Garnett and I would walk through it. Instead of getting kindly acquainted with my mother's boyfriend, I got bad conversation. The apartment was ugly, he said. How much had I declared on last year's income tax return? Wasn't I an adult yet?

He put mirrored sunglasses on and started hauling boxes. So when I said the apartment looked nice with furniture and curtains, that some people praised my ability to make do on a budget, that I was a student, an apprentice, that most of my income was a teaching fellowship, an award, only my mother heard, and even she said we needed to stop wagging our chins and load. I couldn't object anyway because they were moving my furniture he didn't like either. I couldn't see his face as they pulled away. My mom waved—parting, sweet sorrow—as if this was just another Kodak moment in the family annals.

I headed out the next day.

A week before, I'd taken my car to a mechanic and asked him to change the oil, the coolant, the transmission fluid too. The mechanic said transmission fluid was good for the life of the car. "But," I said— and I concede that there's a fine line between being preemptive and meddlesome—"won't new fluid help me shift gears with less friction?" I was about to cross mountains. The mechanic said he, personally, wouldn't bother. But I prevailed and headed west, fluids refreshed, looking like an Okie with a few fragile home furnishings in the back (a lamp with a glass finial and a shade made of flocked celluloid, a picture painted on the back of domed glass), also bedding I'd used to sleep on the floor the night before and would again my first night in Utah, and an ironing board, suitcases, an atlas.

It was a thousand-mile trip. I had time to think about interstate highways not taken.

My thesis advisor had suggested a PhD in rhetoric, a semipractical suggestion since there's always a need for people to teach composition and people to teach people to teach it. Another professor suggested I get a PhD in American studies with an emphasis on women writers, turn expert in a burgeoning field. I could get a degree in creative writing too, not practical since thousands already had these master of fine arts degrees and argued about what they were for: to create artists? to create teachers? To teach, you first had to publish a book. To teach rhetoric or literature, you had to publish too—papers, book chapters—which was a matter of knuckling down, doing research, whereas the how-to of becoming a published novelist or poet seemed to me pie-in-the-sky and vague.

I hoped, in the end, for a stable life.

But there are different levels.

I'd heard since third-grade social studies class that no one is permanently above the plebeian rest of us, that anyone who works hard can become great or rich. But few people do, and so, impatient with barriers that prevent this rise to greatness, we painstakingly mark lines that separate those who have from those who have a little less. But I didn't think about that as I drove. Beyond feeling hurt, then defensive, distant, because my father had told me that if I got another degree he was done with me for good—what did that mean? I wondered—I didn't understand that getting another degree would change me enough to eliminate the last conversational threads connecting me to my family, shred that net forever. I'd never been connected anyway, except to my mother, whose conversational threads now floated, connected to no one, her talk about canned corn and bankruptcy. Besides, I was poor, and jobs I'd be aiming for weren't guaranteed. I was who I was so far, or seemed to be, a black sheep afraid of real work.

I'd applied to PhD programs in rhetoric and literature at good state universities. Schools at the pinnacle of the Carnegie Commission on Higher Education's hierarchy of impressiveness weren't on my radar. I'd studied with just one professor who'd gone to one, an eighteenth-century scholar who spent part of every lecture describing his salad days at his Ivy League school and the big letdown it had been to end up teaching us. I wanted to emulate instead my professors who'd come through on the GI bill, inching forward to the examined life. "Education is not the filling of a bucket but the lighting of a fire," William Butler Yeats. I'd grown up with different words. I once wrote a paper on William Butler Yeats, and over and over I used Wite-Out for this typo: William Butler Yeast.

I could have gone south, studying women writers. I could have gone north, studying rhetoric. I could have gone northwest or southeast. I'd applied to the Iowa Writers Workshop and the University of Iowa, writing in my letters of application that I wanted to earn an MFA in creative writing—gambler's degree, source of joy and sorrow—and a PhD in literature at the same time. I got accepted at both programs but thought hard about writing a thesis and dissertation simultaneously. In the end, I headed to the University of Utah to get one of the brand-new PhDs that let students write creative dissertations. For four years, I'd write fiction but do scholarship on the history of the novel.

Motoring onward, I'd sometimes check the map and glance at states where I didn't go and consider the person I wouldn't become—with a different geographical past, a different deeply mined obsession, a different set of brain-goods on the shelf for times of boredom. The world also churns out aphorisms about how useless education is. But it makes you good company for yourself as you live out fast-flying days and nights until you die, just another human with plights and scrapes in a long line of human plights and scrapes.

I stopped at a truck stop in Wyoming with shower stalls, a big diner, hundreds of semitrucks with sleeping cabs where the drivers catch forty winks. When I got to Utah, someone told me that this truck stop is also famous for prostitutes. I pumped gas, went inside to pay. I glimpsed the diner window, full of lone wolves, and walked back to my car.

The sun had begun to set, the sky dimming, vapor mercury lights buzzing and snapping. Before I got in my car to drive off, I lifted the hood to check the oil. I also looked under the car. Even in shadows I could see strands of thick fluid dripping. I slid underneath—I was wearing one of the ankle-length, sleeveless dresses I'd sewn for this trip, thin cotton marked down to $1.99 a yard, because my car didn't have air-conditioning, and nothing is cooler than a cotton dress—and felt around for the source of the leak: a seam between a pan bottom that connected to a pan top, and bolts holding these together were loose enough that I could twist them with my hand. I was losing transmission fluid. In a matter of miles, I'd have an immobile car in need of repairs that cost more than the car. A voice boomed from above, immanent: "Need help?"

Friend or foe, I wondered from under the car, knowing that all this person could see was my car with its hood propped and my feet in white sandals, Payless ShoeSource, $6.99.

I crawled out, stood up, looked at him—a trucker with a T-shirt, steel-toed boots, a toothpick in his mouth, tattoos before tattoos were hip. Or something like that. It was getting dark, and this was a long time ago. He could go either way, I knew. He was the gentlemanly trucker sometimes celebrated in country song who rides the highway doing right by women and children, or tough enough to do me wrong and never look back. My options were shrinking. In an apologetic voice, I said my car was leaking transmission fluid.

He crawled under my car to look. "Yup, transmission," he yelled, muffled.

He slid back out, stood up, looked at my worldly goods piled in the backseat, a pillow, blankets, the old-fashioned lampshade resting against the window. "You heading somewhere?"

I said, "Salt Lake City." The future, I thought. Rock candy mountain where bluebirds sing. Or at least my last stop before I'd settle and friends would stop being bit players and match each other, become a circle, a unity, and all my selves would match too.

He raised his eyebrows. "That's a ways to go yet. You got family nearby?"

An aunt I barely knew lived four hundred miles the wrong way. I didn't say that. I said, "I'm moving. I'm about halfway there." He looked at the car again, then asked how long I'd been at the truck stop, and I said just long enough to pump gas and pay for it.

He said, "Then I don't think you've lost much fluid. It would have been up in the gears out on the highway. These bolts have just shook loose. Looks like someone put them on and didn't tighten them except by hand—like he plain forgot to go back in with the electric wrench. But why anyone would mess with the transmission pan? Makes no sense."

My idea, of course.

The mechanic had said leave well enough alone. Still, he'd messed up the last step.

"Where you spending the night?" the trucker asked.

"I thought I'd drive into Laramie," I said. The sun was gone now, gone.

He said, "Look, I'll tighten these bolts for you with my wrenches. Then get yourself to Laramie. In the morning, go to a mechanic and tell him to check your transmission fluid level and use power tools to get these bolts fastened down. I know a fair enough mechanic in Laramie." The trucker took out a card and wrote on it. "Tell him I sent you and to fix that transmission pan right." He left and came back with his tool box. When he slid out from under the car, he said, "I tightened them as tight as I could."

"Thank you," I said. What else was there to say?

He disappeared, never to be seen again.

This kindness-of-strangers story matters because, years later, when I'd married a second time, my second father-in-law liked to run the dinner table conversation by asking everyone—his sons and daughters and their spouses; his wife's sons and their spouses; the next generation; even a great-grandchild because one of the granddaughters got pregnant in high school—to each take a turn telling a story on a subject he'd pick. This night he asked us to describe the bravest moment of our lives so far. Someone said when he was in a 7-Eleven during a holdup. Someone else said parachuting. A step-sister-in-law said waiting through her baby's fever. I said breaking down at a truck stop west of Cheyenne in an old car, with no money, lying underneath the car, and hearing a stranger's offer and coming out from under to reckon with it. My father-in-law said, "That felt unsafe?"

I said, "I mean I had to be calm even though I was scared because I'd staked everything on this move." My second father-in-law cut his beef. "Hmm," he said, "I was expecting something about risk, a story about physical valor." I remembered how tense I'd been while driving, gripping the wheel, shoulders sore from teeth-gnashing worry about money, about the car's ability to get me across the continental divide, about bad job statistics for people with PhDs someone had shown me before I'd left Kansas, the pressure to publish in the next few years or forget about a job. "Physical valor, no," I said.

How will we know it's us without our past? John Steinbeck.

My second ex-father-in-law—not as nice as the first, not even close—vanished too.

In the Event of
an Apocalypse

I drove around one mountain range and across another. I kept getting higher, ascension.

The air got thin. My ears popped.

Then my car propelled itself down, gravity in charge, road signs on both sides blurring by. "This must be the place," Brigham Young is known to have said when he and the handcart pioneers arrived in 1846. He'd felt sure because the Wasatch Mountains stand guard to the east, the Oquirrhs to the west, the Traverse Range to the south, the Great Salt Lake a moat across the north and west, geographical barriers keeping outsiders out.

I moved into a tiny duplex, matching shotgun apartments. The other apartment housed the landlord's devout cousin and the cousin's wife. The landlord told me their apartment was identical to mine. "Not a great layout," he said, "because tenants use common walls at the same time." My neighbors and I opened matching front doors at the end of the day, cooked dinners in adjacent kitchens, sat in adjacent living rooms, turned out lights in adjacent bedrooms; in the morning, we scrambled for the last of the hot water in adjacent bathrooms.

These dual apartments might seem symbolic: on the one side, husband and wife; on the other, a misfit typing into the night, quiet typing, clicking. I'd bought a computer when my student loan arrived, chunks of plastic that cost more than I'd so far spent on a car. But no. I didn't want my neighbors' life. And I wasn't sure about my own. My landlord, who'd described himself as "a congenital Mormon, born that way, not my fault," told me the neighbor-wife was nice but to avoid the husband, who'd try to convert me, or shun me. He shunned me, no preamble. We spoke once when he banged on my door to say that leaving my porch light on until eleven the night before had cost him sleep and he hoped I wouldn't make late nights a habit. His eyes flicked over my arms, my sleeveless blouse.

In the grocery store, men sometimes gave me the same once-over, curious but repulsed, because my bare arms, my skirt two inches above the knee, seemed slutty. Mormon women end up with a moderate version of purdah, because clothes cover sacred undergarments with insignia on the nipples, navel, and knees. Both men and women wear these. I noticed telltale ridges beneath clothing. I'd see them—like old-fashioned Victorian underwear—hanging on clotheslines as I walked to school. Salt Lake City was a "monoculture," a professor said during orientation, exceptions being out-of-staters doing doctoral work, skiers, and missionary-converted Tongans on the west side.

Male classmates stared in a different way.

We all lived in one small neighborhood a few miles from campus. The students came from all over, Massachusetts, Ohio, New York, Hawaii, France, California. But only a few of us were studying in the same track, fiction with a secondary focus on history and theory of the novel, "narratology" as a classmate who liked postmodernism and wore a toupee liked to say. But no matter whether you were studying literature, rhetoric, linguistics, creative writing, we were all new to the city and not Mormon. Getting a PhD was enforced proximity. We saw each other in classes by day, at parties at night.

What did I think about marriage now? In a city where bridal shops outnumbered bars, on a campus where the word "covenant" appeared over and over in undergraduate papers I graded, I wondered if I'd taken my vows too lightly. If so, I'd failed in a way I couldn't fathom, because I'd trusted the minister who'd said during our ceremony that the key to marriage is believing this: "I can grow. My spouse can grow. Thus, the marriage grows."

I'd tried that. And spent hours since noting it wasn't enough. My husband had been "mellow," as everyone said. Translation: He didn't like work. No one does. But most of us accept it's necessary. Yet if I'd met someone with aspirations, wouldn't I have had to turn mine into genteel hobbies that fit around the edges of womanly duty? Like all recent divorcées, I'd sworn off marriage. But I wanted it, bosom of family, cozy ideal. Marriages did exist in which women had careers. I read about them in famous people's biographies; I met a few women who lived this life. But it seemed to require money. It didn't happen much in the lower middle class. I applied myself to the life of the mind.

I didn't let my thoughts wander, daydreams. But I night-dreamed, urges beyond willpower. The only other recurring dream I had at the time was about ledgers: long columns recording money spent, short columns recording money earned. But when I dreamed about sex, or the shimmer of desire for it since I'm a staid midwesterner raised to be respectable, I dreamed about the moments before, the premonition of that clumsy tumble toward astonishment. Inappropriately. I dreamed about the husband of a woman I liked. Twice, I dreamed about a seventeenth-century poet who spoke ardently from his grave.

The male graduate students were tense too. We'd all embarked on this elongated run toward a career that might not happen. We'd left behind friends and lovers. Parties were courtship displays, if you consider courtship a biological event and not the subject of a sonnet cycle. The men preened, proving strength by consuming vast amounts of toxins.

The women preened, consumed toxins, awaited. One couple eloped within days of meeting, then fought about whether to divorce or annul. This was the 1980s, free love twenty years old, if not a hundred. I can't speak for the wives of the English Romantics, but for me the sexual revolution made it hard to say No. One classmate asked me out and returned again and again to his pet topic, that we had to have sex because not to was to go through life as if wearing blindfolds. And after the just-once, he spoke to me like I was annoying.

Another graduate student made a case for himself, but he had that toupee, which didn't quite match his remaining hair—this was before balding men shaved their entire heads to reveal, voilà, the phallic head. He said Robert Coover's work was an assault on cliché-ridden templates society imposes on us. He kissed me. He must have thought I had hyperactivity disorder manifesting as arousal because I tilted a lot, obliging him to tilt. I wanted the toupee to slip so he'd take it off. He wouldn't try to go to bed with it on, would he? Fake hair was a template imposed by society. Or maybe I tilted to seem hysterical, uptight. It worked. He stopped, never unveiling his head nor his innermost self.

Next, I met someone who'd finished coursework for a PhD in folklore but hadn't written his dissertation. "Or I'm taking eleven years to write it," he said, wry, self-deprecating. He was tall, ten years older than me. He carried snacks in his sports coat pockets. He lived in a house famous for squalor and good parties. We discussed where we grew up, or where I grew up, because he knew where he grew up, Brooklyn, and it didn't interest him now. He urged me to describe northern Wisconsin customs and jokes. One night he'd cadged tickets to the symphony, where, during intermission, he cadged brownies and asked me to put them in my purse. Afterward, we went to his dissertation director's house—the dissertation director an old friend now, no longer expecting the dissertation.

As we sipped wine, my date asked me to tell Wisconsin jokes. He liked the Ole and Lena jokes, not unlike Tarzan and Jane jokes you might have heard at summer camp when you were ten, jokes where the point is to utter the unutterable, or to spell out how procreation occurs: sex instruction with comedy included. I'd heard these jokes from my sister, who'd married into a Norwegian family and seemed to be cataloging them. When I first told them to the man I was dating, he chuckled, as in *hmm, intriguing*, meantime sifting through his memory for how these jokes correlated to jokes circulating in other subcultures, as though he were doing research while also dating, killing two birds, one stone.

But when he asked me to tell the jokes at the house of the folklore professor, the professor and his wife looked puzzled. I'd sewn a black sateen dress to wear to the symphony, so I felt dressed up but uncouth as I recited, wondering if the professor and his wife thought I thought these jokes were rollicking party banter and not, as my date had said to me, vehicles for the transmission of beliefs from a culturally isolated corner of the Midwest that deserved analysis before they vanished. All well and good, I thought. But Spooner was still there and its inhabitants still told lewd jokes and perhaps would forever.

A date gone this awry might turn out fine if, for example, we could have gone back to my apartment and slipped off my shiny dress and made love like James Stillman and I used to do in Wisconsin, like Max and I used to do in Kansas, where you get into tried and true positions that take you to brief ecstasy. Then we'd relax, agree that the joke-telling had turned awkward. If the sense of intimacy lasted, in time I'd even be able to tell my date he needed to dry clean his sports coats. But the sex was polite, muted. Because he was polite, muted? Because his feelings were? I'll never know. He left afterward because he had to teach at a community college fifty miles away in the morning—by which time I was packing up my laundry to take to the laundromat a block away.

I stood outside my door, locking up, and the devout neighbor's wife came outside. Her husband wasn't with her. She said, "Do you have a new boyfriend?" I must have looked startled. She said, "Don't be embarrassed. I saw he picked you up wearing a jacket, and you had on that beautiful dress. Later, I heard voices in your bedroom." I sometimes heard noise in her bedroom, but I turned up music to drown it out. She said, "God doesn't want us to go through our lives alone, no matter how hard it is to be with someone."

A few minutes later, sorting, loading, measuring detergent, setting some washers on hot with full agitation, others on warm with low agitation, I thought how brute needs get mixed up with tradition, so confusing, and I shut the last lid. I'd gotten picky, having had good sex with Rodney V. Meadow, with James Stillman, with Max, who still phoned me, his voice husky as he said he missed me, which might be true, but he wasn't well traveled and seemed to be angling for an invitation to visit, see the world by way of your ex-girlfriends. Then an extreme sports guy—except no one called them that yet, we called them ski bums, these non-Mormon guys who'd moved to Utah for the mountains and snow and spent warm months hiking and rock climbing—asked me for help with his laundry.

I was relieved to be useful in an uncomplicated way. I explained sorting for color, choosing settings, and how to save money on dryers by taking out lighter pieces first and folding them as the heavy pieces continued to dry. As we waited through wash, rinse, spin, tumble, we noted we were the same age, except I was getting a PhD. "PhD, oh wow," he said. He was an undergraduate, philosophy and environmental geoscience. The double major had slowed him down, he said, as had his job teaching skiing at one of the resorts. With regard to the laundry tutorial, he said, "That was helpful. I'm grateful." He'd been raised in a suburb, in Delaware. I said, "Your mother didn't teach you before you left home?" He said, "It's not easy being green." I thought he meant something about geoscience. He said, "Green like greenhorn. The lesson takes when the pupil is ready."

Several months later on a Friday night, the phone rang, a call from a party a few blocks away. The other woman in the fiction track had told the revelers she was sure I owned a blender because I'd gotten conventional wedding gifts whereas she and her new husband had requested matching motorcycle chaps, a new tent, sleeping bags for winter camping, and I heard laughing, shouting. The guy who'd bedded me and every other single female with his line about how not having sex is like going though life as if blindfolded got on the phone and asked me to bring my blender because he was making margaritas.

Having divorced by age twenty-six was my distinction, in the same

way, for instance, that having a toupee or motorcycle chaps was someone else's. I realized this almost as soon as I got to Utah when I one
day walked to school and a car pulled up, its door swung open, and a
man with pants unzipped—rhythmic juddering, once witnessed, never
to be unremembered—sprayed me and drove off. Flashers flash everywhere, especially in cities. Yet even for a city, Salt Lake had a lot
of pesky sex crime. The paper was always reporting Peeping Toms or
some man who'd masturbated on women's doorknobs.

I had to teach soon, so I hurried to campus, into the restroom, used
soap and water. I went to the big office I shared with other students,
water splotches on my clothes, and my officemates asked what happened, and I explained. I started crying. Embarrassed, I explained the
crying by saying I'd also just that morning realized my ex-husband,
who, according to our divorce decree, was supposed to repay me in
small installments the cost of the cars I'd bought him, hadn't yet sent
any money, and I'd never be able to collect it living here because I'd
only been able to collect it in Kansas by knowing when his band was
playing and going to wake him when he still had cash, and it was sad I'd
never spend that part of my student loans on education now. Or I was
upset about the flasher, deflected crying. One officemate said, "Holy
shit! You're divorced already."

I should have stayed home from the margarita party and worked on
a paper, due in a week, but instead I'd been fretting about the folklore
boyfriend I'd continued to date. Men and women had paired off since
the beginning of time, I thought. Why was it hard now?

I had only an inkling that trouble-with-love wasn't just my confusion—though it was, in part—but also the era's, a slow shift in understanding what wooing and mating would be during a large-scale movement of women into new professions, large-scale movement period,
mobility, not just upward but away from familiar communities where
you date your neighbor's cousin or someone you met at your sister's
wedding, friends serving as dating letters of reference. No wonder arranged marriages persist, I thought. But every time I wondered if my
choices had been affected by factors beyond my control, I resisted.

What did I have if not control? Just secondhand furniture, an old car, and a blender.

I put the blender in a huge purse, went to the party, and met my second husband.

I did this to distract myself. Or to keep options open, avenues to the future.

I didn't marry him that night, but I drank too much and brought him home.

He was the department head's wife's brother's roommate. The department head had moved to Salt Lake City because of the job, and his wife—like Ruth, whither thou goest—followed. Then her brother followed her. Then her brother's college roommate followed.

So I woke up with a short guy who suggested we address the emergency of our hangovers by eating breakfast at a diner, where he said how exhausting he found the parties he went to with his roommate and roommate's sister and brother-in-law, all the people who wanted to tell you what they'd read with a view to pointing out that it was more than you'd read. I countered this by telling him how, in front of classmates, I once said *merlott*, as opposed to *merlot* with a silent *T*, overthinking my pronunciation by first considering that claret, also French but drunk by the English, rhymes with carrot. A pert classmate who dated one of our professors—this wasn't frowned on yet—had corrected me.

My future husband phoned the next day and the next and next.

I canceled plans with my folklore boyfriend, saying I didn't feel good. One effect of free love on women is serial monogamy entered into too rapidly because women are supposed to play the field just long enough to pick a mate. I couldn't sleep with two men; I'd be a whore or vamp. The folklore boyfriend stopped by my apartment. We sat at my kitchen table. I wanted to ask point-blank if I should pick him or a guy he didn't know except as a good outfielder on the intramural team composed of men loosely affiliated with the English Department. I said, "I'd like more certainty you have feelings for me."

Spring sunlight poured through the windows. He had a nice mustache, kind eyes. He needed a slight makeover and a housekeeper. "I'm deeply fond of you," he said. Then he flexed his hands. "Is there something else I should be saying?" At the time I thought I could commit to wanting to love him, that if both of us committed to wanting to, in time we'd love each other. That's possible. But you have to pick a person with the same wanting-it-to-work level who also negotiates differences well, and the two of you have to be hot for each other because that's part of wanting it to work. "I," he said, "love." He paused. "You." He smiled. I flinched. We agreed to meet soon to discuss love.

When he left, I stood in the doorway. He waved. The devout neighbor's wife came out and said, "You broke up with him, right?" I frowned. My kitchen table wasn't near the common wall, not that I'd broken up with him. I thought about telling her she was nosy, but that would mean acting haughty while passing her on the sidewalk each day; I'm not naturally haughty, so I'd have to work at it. She said, "You should. I'm rooting for you to find the right man." I was wondering how this fit, theologically. I was not-converted, damned, but if I found the right man I'd be less damned? She said, "You met someone with more passion. I heard your headboard banging the wall last week and I thought that can't be that old guy." In fact, my future husband was just a few years younger than the folklore boyfriend and his lovemaking style was more athletic, but not better.

I got similar advice from the motorcycle chaps classmate, who'd known her husband a month before they decided to marry. "He was The One," she said. "I knew it right away. You've been dating what's-his-name forever." Another classmate had moved in with an engineering PhD student after six weeks. "We knew immediately," she said, "that what we want to talk about isn't the same, but differences enlarge our world." She left out that the two of them had gotten into huge fights about who had uglier used furniture.

I had a coffee date with my husband #2—though he wasn't my second husband yet, and let's say his name is Chet—and he objected to the fact that we'd had sex once and not again. My indecision had ripple effects. He'd been dating—casually, he said—his roommate's sister's friend, who'd told Chet to choose, and he wouldn't until I did. I started to panic, not about losing Chet, but about how I must seem to the woman Chet had been dating, or actually to her friend, the department head's wife. I imagined the department head and his wife discussing me at dinner as they passed around meat and potatoes.

I'd just handed out flyers in my Freshman English class about the university's counseling center. I made an appointment. A counselor, having seen all varieties of moral blind spots, would have insight, I felt. When I got to the counselor's office—with a big window, the Wasatch Range a jagged cordon across the sky—I saw my counselor was a middle-aged man; I assumed he was Mormon because of his double-knit slacks, the side-part hair. Mormons don't look alike. But rules about tattoos and beards encourage conformity. I looked for the ridges of his sacred garment through his slacks, check. But I believed in higher education. He had a PhD. He'd be trained to counsel non-Mormons too.

I summarized my situation, my sense that neither of these guys was The One, but I felt pressure because of the department head's wife's friend. I was confused, maybe lonely. Life was coupled-up here, I said, not just Utah with its emphasis on brides and progeny, though it was, but the graduate students moved in and out of each other's apartments every time school let out between quarters. None of us had spare time to linger over dating—we settled the romance question fast and got back to work. The dating pool for non-Mormons was finite, I added, like a small town high school where people recirculate. The counselor scrawled on a notepad. He said, "I'm referring you to a psychiatrist who specializes in this disorder." I thought of my wandering grandmother. Was I schizophrenic? I did have fragmented thinking: halfscholarly, half-lusty. The counselor said, "He counsels sex addicts." I'd never heard the term. Most people hadn't yet.

He said, "You'll undergo a program to get over this impulse to escape ordinary stress through meaningless sexual contact. You might need in-patient treatment." I rushed out of the building. I had to cross campus for a seminar on the Victorian novel, where we'd discuss the collective obsession with legitimacy and lineage as a desire for social order that gets mimicked by plot—the end of the story that delivers its message authoritarian and elevated, and scenes leading up to it like minors, dependents, which is to say that the family with its dictatorial clan-head shows up in vestigial shadow-forms everywhere.

My mind was racing as I ran, birds chirping, bees buzzing, trees blooming, branches quivering with pollen, and I bumped into someone and dropped my copy of *Middlemarch*. "Hey, I've haunted the laundromat. I should have gotten your phone number." It was the extreme sports guy. He was handsome, I realized, blinking. But I didn't ski, hike, camp. I said so out loud, apparently. Because he laughed and said, "I'm not looking for that. We could see a movie. When we know each other better, we could take turns cooking each other dinner." Months earlier I might have given him my phone number. Now I had two boyfriends, and—I looked at my watch—in less than ten minutes I'd be sitting in class with that guy I'd had sex with just after I'd moved here, having fallen for a pickup line, also the toupee guy I'd kissed. Maybe I did handle life's ordinary stress with meaningless sexual contact. I said, "I'm in a big mess in terms of my schedule."

His smile faded. "I understand. The PhD, all-consuming."

Love does happen fast. I fell for a house.

After I broke up with the folklore boyfriend, Chet started coming over all the time with clothes for his office job the next day, and I thought I was being cautious, centrist, by thinking about living with him, not marrying him, because pairing off seemed to be a virus everyone had caught. When the quarter ended, I attended housewarming parties for new couples and two weddings. I wanted to live with someone. Or I wanted out of the duplex, its thin wall, its rooms so small and few that, furnished, it felt mazelike. I called ads for two-bedroom houses, and during one call I recognized my landlord's voice. He said, "For you, a discount. Your rent is on time, and you improve the property by living in it."

The house I loved had oak floors, a white fireplace, a living room, dining room, big porch, a bedroom for love and sleeping, another for writing and homework. The street in front was a thoroughfare, and our bedroom looked onto a boarded-up house, but a nice family lived on the other side. Our kitchen window faced theirs; our dining room window faced theirs. On dim days, I'd watch them cook, eat. I felt light-years away from campus and its intrigues. And because I'm enthralled by unused space—ways to fill it, doors leading to the unknown—I loved the basement you got to through an outside entry.

It had a fruit cellar, which Chet equipped with grow lights for seedlings for flowers for the front yard, vegetables for the backyard, and hydroponic pot plants. The rest of the basement was surrounded by five-foot-deep shelves that I assumed were structural ballast. No, the landlord said, they were built to store food, water, fuel. Preparedness for cataclysm—an earthquake, a government takeover, or End Time—was doctrine. Was a government takeover seen as likely? I asked, curious. "That part's probably a holdover from the polygamous days," he said. Souls need food? I asked. All religions are mystery religions, of course. God knows. We don't. The landlord said, "I guess the idea is that the righteous might not get taken right away and would have to duke it out with the left-behinds."

So what got the fighting started?

Chet and I painted the inside of the house, and he got upset because my brushstroke was inefficient. I tried to make light by calling him Paint Marshal. He got upset in the store when I backtracked to pick up a jar of mustard we'd meant to buy, so that he could continue on with the list, the cart, but we were not to separate in the store. I needed to finish my degree fast because he was staying in Utah only for me, he emphasized; he wanted to move ASAP. Basically, we had our first fights, never-resolved, a solid fighting foundation.

Subsequent fights built on that.

But he had a green thumb. He fried food well. He praised my collection of lace curtains—some old, others $6 a panel at Wal-Mart and you launder them on gentle—and the antiques I'd earned out at Garnett's store. He said, "I've wanted a homespun woman, but they're usually dumb as cows. I didn't think a smart one would be interested in me."

I attributed this—he didn't think a smart one would be interested—
to the fact he wasn't tall. Women are biased toward tall men. He also
didn't feel worthy because he'd been raised by a single mother who'd
had to work and sometimes left her kids with ruthless people.

One night, coming back from playing Scrabble at a party, and
we'd drunk wine, and Chet was mad I'd played for the most interesting words, not points, and I temporarily misplaced my appeasement
mindset and told him he was a control freak. He reached across the
seat and hit me. I hit him back. You might think: she showed him,
and that was that. No. I learned not to bother him if I could help it because his first instinct—instilled when he was a child, more beaten on
that beating—was to swing, swing again. He was strong. The advice my
older self has for my younger, or for you, included with the price of this
book, is don't move in with someone if you don't have savings, first and
last month's rent plus deposit. Don't sign a lease. I had to make it work
until the year's end.

That bad fight put the kibosh on the athletic sex.

We were both mad but pretended we weren't as we went to work,
school. I never turned to him at night, and he didn't insist, going to
sleep holding me as tight as a child would.

I had straight As, but I hadn't published. I sent out my stories, each
accompanied by a manila-colored, self-addressed envelope with correct postage so the journal could respond. Chet spent weekdays at
work, where he negotiated easements for oil and gas. I split time between campus and home. I'd be working, making headway, and check
the mail to find, over and over, manila envelopes, form-letter rejec-
tions, no encouraging notes, mixed in with the bills. Some of the bills
were Chet's from out of state, way past due.

Before we moved in, I'd studied our expenses. I earned less than
he did but was used to being frugal. So I'd proposed we split rent and
utilities fifty-fifty. We should have been fine. But he always wanted
something, a housetop satellite dish or, if not that because, shrewlike,
I'd objected, a new TV. Or he hadn't paid his half of the rent when he
spent $400 on exotic tulip bulbs because, with winter coming, he was

planning for spring. He said, "The trouble with you is that you've never had money and don't know how to spend it. You're what we call penny-wise and pound-foolish." I'd studied him too, making sure he wasn't like my first husband, too calm, lazy. Chet's impatience, his pushy way of insisting, meant he'd be forceful about earning money, I'd felt. But the money problems got worse. Waitress experience, my mother had said, you'll use all your life.

One night I came in from the restaurant at 11:30 p.m., later than usual, because my friend Shen and her boyfriend had come to the restaurant and I'd waited on them and we'd visited a while before I cleaned my station, wiping away grease and food on cabinets, tables. The end of a shift is hours of carrying other people's dirty dishes while congealing food spills on your clothes. I opened the back door to the house and saw that Chet had cooked dinner, fried sardines and fried canned oysters, according to the empty, smelly cans on the counter, the stove covered with spatters. And what had required a colander? I wondered. He tended to use one without a sink. He'd dumped something into a colander over the stove, then thought twice because murky liquid trailed across the floor.

I woke him to say that when I'd left for work the kitchen was spotless.

It's a bad idea to wake a sleeping person with a history of anger management issues to say anything at all. He hit me. I kept yelling. My yelling is querulous and tremolo, not commanding, maybe excruciating in the way silent whistles are to dogs. Chet swung again. I ducked. My head banged into the wall, crumbling the old plaster. Then he started breaking, one at a time, fragile home furnishings, all of which were mine, treasured.

I ran out the door and drove and drove.

After an hour, I passed the house. The lights were out. I parked on a street Chet wouldn't drive down on his way to work, walked home, lifted the basement door, and crept downstairs to the well-swept basement, its cheery furnace humming, lay on one of the five-foot ledges where emergency supplies should be stored for the righteous duking it out with the left-behinds, a situation that, if I meant to be thematic, made me not left-behind, not righteous, but one of the supplies for someone who was, I thought confused, dozing.

Through the old-fashioned floor registers, I heard the alarm go off, 6:30 a.m. Chet made coffee in the last tidy corner of the kitchen. He had to work at 8:00. I had to teach at 9:30. The new phone Chet had bought trilled. I sat up carefully, so bills and change in my apron wouldn't shift, jingle. Chet answered the phone, then said: "Top of the morning to you, Shen. No, she's at school already." He was trying hard to sound upbeat, normal. At parties he sometimes paced with his hands in his pockets, whistling. "Would you like to leave a message?" He wouldn't write it down, he said, because we had one of the new answering machines, and Shen should feel free to call back and talk to that.

That night, when he asked where I'd gone, I said I'd used my tips for a motel. I was too cheap to spend a night's worth of earnings to sleep in dirty clothes in a motel, but he didn't know me well enough to know that. He washed the dishes. I cleaned the stove, mopped. We swept up the broken knickknacks. He glued the frame of an antique picture he'd thrown, and he spackled crushed plaster. Three months until the lease was up, I told myself.

But I didn't have the money yet—no first and last month's rent plus deposit.

Then my mom and her boyfriend, husband now, visited on their way to another scouting expedition in Arizona. I'd saved time to spend with them, but they arrived a week late.

They stayed up every night until dawn.

Chet and I lay awake side-by-side, listening to my stepfather wrenching the ice cube trays, walking around in clickety-clack cowboy boots, saying, "Hon, do you think I should go out in this goddamn town and find more ice?" He'd gotten thrown out of the state-owned liquor store that afternoon for threatening a clerk. This was after I'd come home from class to the two of them waiting to see the sights, and

I should have been grading or writing, but I was too tired, and I tried to be nice for my mother's sake, thinking they'd leave soon, and my step-father stared and said: "I'd like a job that lasts three hours a day."

Lying in bed on the fourth night, I pictured my stepfather's boot heels like hooves on the wood floor, my hooved stepfather upright, ambulatory, mixing drinks, and Chet said: "You'll have to tell them to leave." Chet would be at work by the time they woke, he added, so I should tell them. Next to each other in the dark, scared and sleepless, Chet and I quietly had sex for the first time in months. Who knows why? Perhaps not having a mother or father to confide in, a home to go back to if life turned to shambles, made me lonely. I wanted someone. I wanted a replacement family, my goal, my target. Chet was nearby.

The next day, I told my mother and stepfather that Chet and I were having trouble getting our work done. My mother said, "But you're good at school. You'll be fine." I said, "We can't sleep with you party-ing all night." They packed and left. My mother waved, tearful. I never saw my stepfather again except in his casket. I talked to my mother on the phone but didn't see her until he'd died, years and years later. I'd broken a big rule. I'd disregarded generational rank, failed to respect my elders, by sending them away.

I was pregnant.

"You're shitting me," Chet said, beatific. "After just the one time?"

I can't logically explain my joy, my newfound purpose. I'd watch the Mormon neighbors (mother, father, sister, brother) through our matching gold-lit windows. Not having this baby was unthinkable. Be-ing unmarried while pregnant was unthinkable. I was raised to think so. But Salt Lake City exerted its own pressure. I could imagine being an unmarried mother better than I could imagine crisscrossing the city, pregnant, no ring, forced into small talk with cashiers, bank tell-ers, my students. It would be easier to say I was divorced with children, sad facial expression, than to say I'd never married at all. Even a dud husband was better than no husband, I reasoned, someone to doze on the sofa when I left to study or work. I didn't want to give up on my

PhD, or I might for a few discouraged hours now and again, but I owed so much in student loans I couldn't repay them without a good job. I needed to finish the degree, earn a living, support this child.

You don't plan a miscarriage, of course. You plan a wedding.

Days before ours, I was at the restaurant. I'd picked up shifts because we needed money. The midwife had said that many women bleed during the first trimester. Still, she sent me for an ultrasound, bad news. Now I was having mild contractions, nothing to keep me from work or school yet, and I couldn't afford to quit or get fired because Chet was already fired again. But I wasn't sleeping, stunned, carrying a baby that was not the quick but the dead. The other waiters protected me from the chef's wrath by keeping an eye on chores I'd space out. Then, cutting baguette, I sliced off a slab of my finger, still dangling.

I wrapped my hand inside linen napkins and bar towels, turning red fast now, and a customer drove me to the ER, explaining to the triage person that he wasn't my husband. A nurse made a tourniquet, stanched the bleeding, and called Chet. We sat in the ER for hours because a man in the next stall was having a heart attack, and doctors tried to revive him. When they couldn't, and he lay dead on the other side of the curtain, a doctor sewed my finger back together, did a pelvic exam, and gave me pills to hasten contractions.

It takes a specific kind of courage to call off a wedding, and I didn't have it. My finger was still wrapped up. I felt like a broken, half-built something moving along an assembly line. Fellow students arrived to witness our vows in front of our fireplace, to eat cake in our dining room. They disregarded basic writing advice—avoiding clichés and mixed metaphors—and said that star-crossed lovers reach a tipping point and the tide turns.

After this deep-in-winter wedding, Chet started working again. I sat alone in the house, thinking next year, my last in the PhD program, was hard to look forward to now. The only person close to feeling as sad as me about the miscarriage was Chet. So, for a few weeks, he understood me better than anyone else could. How did it matter if I wasn't blissfully married? Most people aren't. Exotic tulips pushing through snow cannot console me, I thought, remembering Theodore Roethke's "Elegy for Jane." Or they must have consoled me for a moment, because one day I looked through the window and saw a stranger glance around furtively and pick the best one, aubergine and yellow stripes, and I thought it would be a year, or never, before I saw another like it again, and I felt terrible again.

But I set goals for myself, finishing a draft of my dissertation, a collection of stories that had been rejected twenty or thirty times each by high-level, mid-level, and low-level magazines and journals, and I'd send them off together as a book manuscript, by midsummer, I decided—not that I expected anything but rejection, but working down, down a list of options is helpful because just when you think you're out you'll find one more.

Most people who praise Utah praise mountains. I praise the autumn, a lull during which the illusion of rebirth by way of fresh notebooks and sharp pencils lasts three perfect months. Chet and I had argued badly just once more when the prospect of being a father after losing his job had turned Chet angry that I'd left the vacuum on when I ran to take food out of the oven and I should have switched it off and saved the rug under it, Chet had said. I'd felt testy too, rolling my eyes. But sitting together in the ER had made Chet, if not my helpmate, a relative. Family is taxing, yes, I thought. And you can run away like my wandering grandmother or hang on like my taskmaster grandmother. Covenant, I thought, looking outside at the rundown Mormon neighborhood, boxy houses in rows.

I was teaching a class, not taking classes, except Immersion Spanish—starting from scratch for advanced proficiency in a foreign language, since the department wouldn't accept Old English, in which I already had moderate proficiency, because studying it was out of fashion now. Our department with its recent hires from Yale and Harvard was new-fashioned. I studied for my exams in the spring, comprehensive exams on 280 books, lasting four days, six hours a day, or five, counting the last two-hour oral exam.

When Chet came home for lunch, I'd put aside my work, the schedule I'd made for myself: I'd read a book a day. This meant revisiting and taking notes on books I'd already read, reading and taking notes on books I hadn't yet read—sometimes a short, congenial book; sometimes a short, difficult book; sometimes a nineteenth-century novel for which I'd roll over remaining hours from the short-book days to read these huge books fast, aggressively, my heart pounding as I searched for passages to unlock deep understanding. I was also waiting tables, and one night I got summoned to the phone, no calls allowed. The head waiter thrust the receiver at me: "Your husband. He says it's serious."

Chet said, "How's it going, hey? You won the Flannery O'Connor Award."

He was talking about a competition for book manuscripts. Many story writers enter it, hundreds of entrants a year. When I'd mailed my manuscript from the airport post office at 11:30 p.m. on the last possible day, I'd told myself this was an exercise in meeting deadlines. Winning meant one first place only. The winner is published with big fanfare—not to be confused with being for sale on the paperback book rack at Rexall Drug.

This was Chet's idea of a practical joke, I supposed. He'd driven me to the airport post office. I cared too much. The mail had already come before I'd left for work. But, no, only the submitters of rejected manuscripts get letters. The winner gets a call.

The director of the series had called and asked for me, and Chet hadn't told him to talk to the answering machine. Chet had jotted down a number so I could call back in the morning. When the director told Chet I'd won, Chet told him I hadn't published hardly at all, just poems, not my stories, which had been rejected everywhere. The director conceded they were unusual, yes, that one at a time they might seem rough-hewn and unskilled, as opposed to subtly wrought in an imitation-of-blue-collar-life way. But all together, he told me on the phone the next day, they comprised a world, an iconography. They were shrewd, feisty. Nice, I thought, exulting. No one before had said anything so pleasant.

I'd made bad decisions, moving in fast with Chet, for instance. But I've had good luck. This prize was luck, not that I didn't work hard, but most people do. And who judges a contest, and what writing he'll like, and who will win is arbitrary—a windfall leading to future windfalls. But before I could think of windfalls, a professor said that since I had an award-winning book in press and would be graduating in June, I should hit the job market. "You won't do well, but it will be good practice for next year." Most new PhDs need at least a year of trial-run job interviews, he explained, before they get an offer.

So one day a week, I read ads and submitted applications. If I looked interesting, a department would ask for more material. If I looked interesting after that, I'd have made the cut from maybe three hundred applicants to ten and get interviewed in a hotel at a national convention between Christmas and New Year's; I'd pay for that trip. If I made the cut after that, I'd travel to a two-day interview on campus, paid for by the interested university.

Chet had a credit card left from the days before he was in trouble with the IRS and banks in Houston—this was why he'd moved to Utah— and he paid that bill on time every month. If I got requests for interviews at the conference, Chet said, he would charge my plane ticket, and we'd pay that back slowly. I didn't have my own credit card yet because this was before banks gave credit to students. I got calls for interviews at the conference.

This might sound like an ideal time for me to have removed myself from the marriage. But we were newlyweds. A lot happened fast. Interviews could lead to a job, money. So I shelved conjecture about good and bad love until this busy spell was over.

When I got to the conference, I consulted a notebook in which I'd taped a subway map, a conference map, notes I'd taken about the universities interviewing me. Fourteen. "Fourteen," my professor said, "no way! Well, you'll get just one or two interviews on campus."

During the first interview, I had a frog in my throat. I worried compulsively that I'd forgotten to hook my blouse at the back of the neck, a pearl button with a loop, and as I answered a question my hand flew involuntarily to check—it was hooked—and the professors interviewing me jumped, then becalmed themselves, assuming, I guess, I had an itch. But my answers were logical. I'd written out questions I imagined I might be asked, trick questions, hard questions, obvious questions, and composed my answers, edited for clarity, and committed them to memory using tricks I'd developed memorizing Luther's Catechism when I was twelve, and the wine list and daily specials when I was twenty-nine. When I'd pause to access my mnemonic triggers, I'd look bemused but not clueless.

I had one last interview the morning before I flew home. Tired, woozy, I dragged myself to it and answered the only question for which I hadn't prepared an answer. My old personality seeped out. I cussed, saying, "It's bullshit that savvy readers don't look for causality. A story is one thing after another, a chain that teases out the desire for cause-and-effect answers to life's big questions, and since the point of art is to give us what life can't, even sophisticated readers crave clear-cut causes and effects, phony effects, resolution." I stared at the gray-haired men on the edges of their chairs staring back as if I were an opinionated trained seal. "In life, though," I said, "there are flukes, happenstance."

I had eight calls for interviews on campus.

In January, the landlord stopped by and said he was selling the house and we could have first shot, no down payment. I'm not clear what instigated what, chicken or egg, but Chet started asking people what they'd heard about cities where I had interviews, reported dire details, pressed me to bow out and pick up classes around Utah like my old folklore boyfriend did. But Chet hated Utah. He'd wanted out. I didn't ask what was wrong in a wifely, patient way. I said I wasn't staying in Utah just to buy a house. And I couldn't consider Chet's doubts for long. I was overscheduled, reading a book a day as I traveled.

I flew to Nevada one sunlit day; to Colorado on a sparkling white day; to North Carolina on a balmy day; to Cleveland, where a professor, assessing my worth while also convincing me of the job's worth, pulled back his office drapes to show me his splendid lakefront view. Loading docks. Smokestacks. I didn't understand that, in urban terms, this was attractive. I felt nostalgic for cattails, lily pads. I lay in my hotel room that night and pretended I was home, and that didn't help. I pretended I was in my childhood bed in Spooner, and that didn't help. I pretended I was on the pier in front of the vanished summer cottage, sunshine and the sluice of waves calm, restorative, and I started to sleep but not long, sitting up and thinking of myself on the basement ledge in Utah, how I'd felt wrongly safe there, unlocked, open to the world. Then I got out of bed and looked out the window at Cleveland's highrises lit like checkerboards and thought: I'm all over the map here.

I flew to Washington state during a squall, and this was the department that had been my last woozy interview at the conference, and the professors must have decided I was fun, or they were. On the last night they took me to a Robert Burns festival, where we drank whiskey and ate haggis. In the morning, at the airport, they waved as if saying so long, see you soon, and my journey was uneventful until it came time to land. A storm had settled into the Valley as if in a bowl, and we circled, people vomiting into their little bags.

When we landed at last, I hauled my suitcase through the airport and passed a guy sleeping next to a duffel bag and pair of skis, and he opened his eyes and smiled. The extreme sports guy, I thought, who'd seemed so nice with his talk of studying, dinner, laundry, movies, and I'd failed to notice in time, and now I wouldn't live in Salt Lake City long, assuming I passed my comprehensive exams, also the foreign language exam on which I'd so far scored high enough for only moderate proficiency. Then he shut his eyes, and I realized it might not be him. I'd seen him just twice. Ski bums look alike. Besides, I was married to Chet, waiting curbside, irritated at another late-night airport pickup.

The next morning I had calls to make. Though I had two more interviews, and good times in Washington notwithstanding since the salary was low, I had offers, the most high-profile one from a department that wouldn't give me more time to decide because they had their second choice waiting. I accepted that job quickly, no chitchat. I had to return to studying. We were all studying—the classmate with the toupee, the classmate with the motorcycle chaps, the classmate who slept with the professor, the classmate with the overused seduction line. I wasn't behind yet, I thought, the house turning dimmer, light buried behind clouds and falling snow. I called the professor with the lakefront office in Cleveland. I wouldn't be taking the job, I said. He seemed amazed. "Really?" Another life I wouldn't try on. And I didn't want him to feel bad he lived in a gloomy city, I thought, though it was perhaps nice in spring. He said, "May I ask where you accepted a job?"

Snow was falling in clumps, and people were driving to work in front of my house, lines and lines of headlights grinding toward downtown jobs. Then I heard a thud, and all at once the room was lit up. A car had slid off the street, crashed onto the porch, its headlights like floodlights; I froze. I looked out the window and saw a terrified woman's face in a windshield ten feet away. I said to the Cleveland man, "We're having a blizzard, and someone has crashed into my house." He probably thought I was lying or crazy.

I hung up, went outside, brought the woman in, called a tow truck, sat her down at my dining room table, and offered her coffee. Being Mormon, she said no, did I have cocoa, and she thought she'd been in my house before. "Maybe," I said. Who knows who used to live here? Next, she said I was her second-cousin's niece. "I'm sure of it, positive." She looked at the room this way and that, then noticed the neighbor's lighted dining room, not very different from mine, and said, "Oh. Everything is starting to look alike." Happy families are all alike, I thought, panicked, because I hadn't read *Anna Karenina* yet. Maybe mildly unhappy families too. The woman and I waited for the tow truck to arrive, and the woman's daughter too. "The poor dear," the daughter whispered, bundling her mother out the door. "She hit the gas exactly when she should have hit the brakes."

Serfs and Landlords

Chet got to Greensboro before me and found a house with two front porches: one open, an invitation to stop by for sociability and a glass of sweet tea; the other screened with a door that locked, a darkened box passersby strained to see inside. In Utah, he'd run out of work. His car was leased. He gave it back to the company and drove a U-Haul truck, towing my tiny, new Subaru I'd bought when a driver had hit my old car, totaled it, and I'd used the insurance money for a down payment and signed my first promissory note.

I spent the rest of the summer in Utah at my friend Shen's, bumming rides to and from work, where I waited tables, including on graduation day, fathers and mothers proudly pointing out the honoree. Once, taking an order for a jolly family, I said I'd graduated that day too—I'd skipped the ceremony, its pricey fees for cap and gown—and the mother politely asked what degree I'd earned. I said a PhD, and she looked upset until I told her I had a real job, but it didn't start for a few months and I needed money. The graduate's father said, "Can we get another photo, this time with the waitress with a PhD?"

Why Chet wanted to stay married is guesswork.

Why I stayed married is guesswork too. I've never been good at saying No, and I don't mean No to sex, though sometimes that. I'd had trouble telling white-shirted missionaries No I don't want to join the Mormon Church. I'd had trouble turning down job offers. So I never thought about telling Chet we should split up before we're trapped together on the other side of the country. Saying No might be everyone's problem, but women are first girls who, like boys, can't disagree with parents, and then they're wives-in-training—that scramble to be a good sport, a salt of the earth. My dad once said, tautological advice when I was an unattached female of the species: "Don't say no. It's negative."

Or I didn't want to move alone again, long haul and nerve-wracking tight budget.

When at last I flew to Greensboro and Chet drove me from the little airport to the little house, he told me he'd impressed our new landlord, who was also the former mayor. The landlord had said, "Son, when your wife gets here, I want to take you to dinner at my country club." I said, "Really? He takes his tenants out to dinner?" Chet said, "He saw something of himself in me, I suppose, and I played into that." Played into it for what? I wondered. "He gave us a rent discount?" Chet said, "I'm making business contacts." I nodded.

At the rounds of orientations, I met other women professors, all hired in the last few years because women now had PhDs, and the new view was that female students—over half the student body—have different research interests, and these students need mentors. Chatting with recently hired women, I noted that their husbands hadn't found work.

One husband who used to be a CEO took watercolor classes now, his wife said. She was glad to have him out of the house because he'd gotten prickly, scheduling the laundry, rearranging dishes in cupboards. Another picked up part-time work. If one spouse moved for another's job, the spouse who'd followed was likely to be unhappy. Yet Chet had never had a career in the way these husbands did, I told myself. He'd have options.

Chet revised his résumé—not exactly untruthfully—by describing his freelance work as owning businesses. His last run of work in Utah had been contract work. In Houston, he'd freelanced during the oil boom, but not steadily, as his mother had intimated when she'd visited us in Utah: "I'm so glad he's stopped selling pot to cover expenses."

One of her other sons was an alcoholic. Another was a police officer, suspended. Another was a deadbeat dad. Her stepchildren were dentists, architects, businessmen, or married to these and working in professions from the "What I Want to Be When I Grow Up" checklist for girls: Mother, Nurse, Secretary. My mother-in-law had been stranded without child support herself, so she was sympathetic to the ex-wife of the son who was the deadbeat dad. This former daughter-in-law had since married money. Marrying money had been my mother-in-law's strategy too. Her husband made money but spent a lot, having pulled himself up by his bootstraps to escape a childhood so dire he craved luxury.

Because Chet seemed sad, edgy, I invited him to the appointment where I made my retirement and insurance decisions. I chose the cheapest health insurance, since we were young. I put the minimum into retirement because we had debt. Then Chet said I should pick the best life insurance. This seemed inconsistent. We were young, as we'd agreed.

I said so. Chet looked testy. The human resources aide had already said how unusual it was for the employee's spouse to come, but nice, she added, that he was taking such an interest. Now she gave us a quizzical look. I signed on, reasoning that, if I were a man and Chet a woman, good life insurance would be the responsible choice. We drove home. Chet looked around, glum, and said he'd never have moved here if not for me.

I might have used multiple job offers to get a better salary, but I'd been flummoxed to have offers at all; I'd worried about jinxing them. And now my name had been released to a mailing list. Or it was a new era in banking. Credit card offers arrived. I threw them away, but Chet needed credit to start a business, he insisted. I wasn't afraid of him.

Or maybe I was afraid for ten minutes here or there, and then I'd leave until he calmed down.

Or it's easy to say so now. But in Utah I could have moved out if I'd taken time off from classes—forgoing my stipend, explaining my predicament to the director of the program, staying in someone's guest room, and bargaining with my landlord. Yet I didn't because I had my work that, if I executed it well and on time, might one day be remunerative, and my love life had nothing to do with that. So I'd had work, and Chet had me. In Utah, I wasn't exactly remunerative for Chet, but I'd been pleasant enough, or at least he'd liked the way I tamed life: curtains, nagging reminders to tidy up and pay bills.

I didn't want him to hit me, of course, so he got his way when I didn't have the patience to argue, leave the house, then start the argument over again. Or the time. I'd come home from teaching—papers to grade, books waiting on my desk—and he'd want to talk. Impatient, I'd lose my temper. I shouldn't have raised my voice. He shouldn't have raised his hand. Most of the time he stopped himself, but not always. By today's standards, using one-size-fits-all diagnostics, he was abusive. But I never thought his anger was my fault. I never felt helpless, or not for long. I had routes out, more than he did. I was outmatched physically. He was outmatched verbally. Years later, he'd be diagnosed with panic disorder so crippling he'd no longer be able to self-alleviate with tantrums.

But I didn't know that then. Our arguments escalated. Unseemly.

I was the youngest professor in the department—the Doogie Howser professor, a student said. The director of graduate studies lived across the street, the dean three doors down.

Seemly mattered.

One night Chet and I were shouting about credit cards, windows raised for fall breezes, and the phone rang. It was Sally, a next-door neighbor who was more like me than anyone else on the street because, though Sally and her husband owned their small house, her husband worked two blue-collar jobs. She was pregnant a third time, a nice surprise, she'd said, yet her husband looked weary and dismal when I saw him: coming, going.

I answered the phone and Sally said: "Are you all right?" I was, I said. She asked again, same phrase, mounting intensity, a little thrill of excitement, a new lease on life, a hobby: me. I mean she sounded happy to be on the phone. I wasn't. I wanted to shut the windows, get back to grading, and I didn't want to discuss the credit card argument with Sally.

Perhaps she saw me as a twin-friend because her husband worked eighteen hours a day and was tetchy when he came home, upset about how she spent money, she told me. She started inviting me over in what she saw as my free time. But I'd be grading. Writing. I wouldn't get tenure if I didn't publish another book—though this hadn't been true for the low-paying job in Washington, I thought wistfully, remembering those fun professors, but of course we'd be busy if we were colleagues, no time for whiskey and haggis.

One afternoon I came home from watching Sally's children while she went to the ob-gyn, and Chet was pressing dress slacks for dinner at the country club. He'd grown up doing odd jobs at a country club in Houston, so he helped me look through my closet to choose what to wear. In Spooner, we had just a golf club—people who paid annual greens fees—but anyone could drink at the golf club bar. I'd also had no time to sew and hadn't yet adjusted myself for North Carolina, adventitious protective coloration, which was bright, neon, I realized in the country club dining room where I felt out of place in my gray dress with matching cardigan. I met the landlord's wife, in her lime-green shell and skort, and the couple joining us, a stockbroker and his wife, in her orange, lock-knit sheath.

The men talked about workers at our landlord's factory. They talked about the senate race, a black former mayor running against the old, white incumbent. Neither the stockbroker nor the landlord admired the old, white incumbent. "But that doesn't mean I'd vote for a black man," the stockbroker said, ordering a drink from a black waiter. "Not that I'm against civil rights, but I draw the line when it comes to hand-outs." I opened my mouth to object to the illogic, not to mention bad manners, yet I had no idea what to say. Chet kicked me under the table, a signal not to say.

The stockbroker's wife turned to Chet and said, "And what do you do, pray tell?"

Chet started to explain what he used to do, but there were no oil pipelines in North Carolina. She looked bored. "What about you?" I asked, changing the subject. She was an interior designer, she said. Her husband said, "She shops with her friends, who sometimes take her advice." She slapped him playfully. Chet was still talking about work he used to do, verifying himself as an earner. The stockbroker frowned and asked Chet why he'd moved to North Carolina. Red-faced, Chet said, "I moved for my wife's career."

Our landlord, named Wyatt, said, "That's right. He's a stand-up fellow."

The stockbroker's wife looked at me. "Oh my. What's your job then?"

I said I was a professor.

She said she'd met her husband at the university where I taught. She made that old quip about earning her MRS. "So how do you all know Wyatt then?" Having missed cue upon cue, I said, "He's our landlord." Everyone at the table went silent. Nearby, diners murmured, clinked. I made a joke: "Every day we collect straw for Wyatt. What he doesn't need, we use to thatch our roof." Everyone laughed, relaxing. "Cute," the stockbroker's wife said.

First semester, I went to campus five days a week. I lost a lot of time walking a mile there and home again, stepping around puddles and, once, onto a big rat that ate poison in someone's garage, then staggered out to the sidewalk to die. I was used to field mice, not rats. I was jumpy, besides. This was the peak of the crack epidemic in the South Atlantic states with a parallel uptick in crime, a woman abducted on campus on a weekday midmorning even. But I'd never before lived in a city, not counting Salt Lake City, which doesn't count, so I tried not to act like a rube and kept it to myself that I felt scared.

I walked because I couldn't afford the campus parking permit, $375. And most professors had schedules that put them on campus just Tuesday/Thursday or Monday/Wednesday/Friday. I made an appointment with my department chair to ask for a better schedule because I needed time to work on my next book. One of the recently hired women had published only short pieces, which would have been enough for tenure four years earlier when she'd been hired, but times change, so many PhDs, professors to spare. She'd been too servile, she told me, saying yes to niggling requests that had derailed her schedule, and now she was back on the job market, interviews at the big convention after Christmas.

Chet and I spent Christmas at a hunting camp down a dirt road in Texas—putting the plane tickets on one of my new credit cards, $3,000 credit line each. Misjudging his projected income, my father-in-law had lost the big fancy house with the stairwell just like Tara in *Gone with the Wind*. I helped cook for Chet's brothers and spouses, Chet's stepsiblings and spouses, Chet's nieces, nephews, great-nephew, and crazy grandma, who'd socked away money and gave my mother-in-law the hunting camp for a place to live.

The furnace broke. My father-in-law made a fire outside and brought buckets of coals inside for warmth, reliving his bad childhood, my mother-in-law whispered, explaining his foul mood. The pipes froze, no baths. Chet's brothers talked about living with the crazy grandma, how she used to hit them, then lock them outside. She followed me around with her walker, lenses in her glasses so thick they were gray, milky, and said: "Bet you would have liked to ride in my Cadillac when I went ninety, hey." Or: "You know what they call a nigger in a Plano? A Plano nigger." At night she'd go back to her warm cottage, and we slept in our winter coats, eight to ten people a room, most of them snoring.

I was tired when I got back in January and went to see my department head. But before I could ask about a schedule that would let me work at home at least two days a week, he asked if I'd reviewed my fall evaluations—forms filled out by students about how effective the professor is. I hadn't yet, I said, worried that I was negligent already, scolded. I'd had good evaluations in the past, but I'd taught only Freshman English. Now I was teaching graduate classes, upper-division classes, and supervising my especially self-doubting teaching assistant, whose parents had asked to meet me to ascertain if a master's degree was right for their daughter, and the question that had nagged them most was whether she might still get married. "Good," the father said, relieved.

The department head smiled and said, "Your evaluations are great." But when I asked about my schedule, his smile vanished: "No." A male professor hired at the same time as me had a Tuesday/Thursday schedule, I knew. I didn't say that. I stared at the tile floor with black heel marks, easy to remove with a bit of oil, then a swipe of Windex. I said, "I teach classes with heavy grading loads, and I agreed to supervise that teaching assistant, which you described as a favor to the department. Now I'm asking you for a favor." He must have been shocked I hadn't left the room yet. I was shocked. I'd said No to his No. My heart raced. My department head said, "Hmm, good point. And we don't want to get a reputation for using up and spitting out our new hires. I'll arrange something."

I walked home, stopping at a little grocer's to buy dinner. Chet was out of state with the car. After listening to him for three months describe the business he'd start, how he'd one day take it public, sell stock, and I'd meanwhile pay the minimum on our monthly bills and we'd have $75 left for food, I told him to go tell Wyatt he was looking for work. Chet got mad. Did I not understand that Wyatt was in textile manufacturing and Chet was not? I saw Sally through the window, so I pulled the shade. I said, "Wyatt knows people." Chet said, "You'll turn my résumé into a hash." Chet did go see Wyatt, though, and now Chet was staying in Georgia for weeks at a time and negotiating power easements.

I passed Ginna's house. She was new to town, having moved here, post-divorce, from a naval base in Virginia. I'd met her one day at the grocer's as we'd chatted about coupons and produce, and she'd invited me over to show me an article that detailed Greensboro's crime rate. Ginna had beaten back a would-be rapist with a hairbrush in her den, she told me. She repeated the story again and again as I said, "Thank God you scared him off," or "Yes, I've heard of victims not remembering how the assailant looked." I doubted her story and felt guilty for doubting it. But her fear rubbed off on me, and I started noticing grisly crimes: a guy who'd microwaved his roommate's body parts; a house-painter who thought a client was uppity, put her in a septic tank, and shot her.

It's natural to want friends, and I scanned the landscape for possibilities. The male professor hired the same time I was lived in a house I passed on my walks to and from school, a house his parents had paid for, he said one rainy afternoon when he'd invited me in for dinner—lentils and cabbage, jug wine—and we discussed his literary analysis by way of Karl Marx, also by way of French and Raven's bases of social power, which I vaguely remembered from Intro to Communication: *reward power*, the power to confer positives, and *coercive power*, the power to create negatives, the power of the otherwise powerless.

At work, colleagues were friendly but formal. One talked to me about travel and opera. When he realized I'd never traveled, just moved, that I didn't know opera, he stopped. It would have been easier to befriend graduate students because I'd been one recently, but I taught them, so I kept a distance. I'd run across an undergraduate I'd taught in the fall but wouldn't again, the one who called me Doogie Howser—his name was Kip, and he'd see me walking in bad weather and offer me rides. I'd decline. One day, the winter sun sinking fast, he pulled over, opened his door, quoted a Dylan Thomas poem we'd read for class: "*Rage, rage against the dying of the light*. Hey, accept a ride already."

Late at night, I sometimes got long-distance calls from friends fading into the past. Chet had bought a new phone that was also a fax machine, and I was supposed to answer it while pretending to be Chet's secretary ("You have reached Seismic Solutions"). A woman from my PhD program, who'd taken a job in South Carolina, called once a week to tell me my job was better, my life too, she said, because I was in love, not lonely. If I said my life was harder than it seemed, she asked for details, and I said, "Chet has been unhappy here. He had trouble finding work." But he'd always had trouble finding work. He'd always been unhappy. "Something's off-kilter," I said. I felt like his mother or older sister. My friend wasn't married, but she wanted to be. "Don't get stuck on a Prince Charming fantasy," she said. "That's buying into normative gender stereotypes."

One night I got a call from my college roommate from Oconomowoc, and she told me James Stillman was dead. I'd like to report that the sudden weight of this knowledge—he'd been thrown from a car, and the car landed on him—gave me insight about life, how we spend it alone, or how we spend it with others, suppressing our private objections to public truths, some brand-new wisdom about belonging, not belonging, the knitting together, the untangling. I worried instead about sounding appropriate. I listened to the details of James's death and expressed vague regret. Was I too sad to say so? Or afraid of dying myself? I felt haunted, I decided, and I couldn't afford not-sleeping, the feeling that, in spite of my locked windows and doors, I wasn't safe.

Chet sometimes came home for long weekends, and I told him I was afraid, yet I hadn't been in the past. Living in cheap housing, I used to hear night-noises and not mind that locks are illusions. In Kansas, the lock on the outside door was meant for a bedroom or bathroom, the door itself hollow, with a hole in its veneer where someone had kicked it. Chet listened to me as he checked the toner in his fax machine, organized the business cards and stationery he'd had printed, put his new TV on top of the not-yet-old TV. He'd bought a TV to use in Georgia because the ones in motel rooms were bad. He'd joined a gym too. He was earning money but putting it all back into his business, he said. When I said that a TV wasn't a business expense, he said he gave up a thriving career in Utah for me, and I realized he now believed the mostly invented sections of his résumé.

Spring was muggy, and the only air conditioner was in the living room. At night, I wanted to turn it off and open bedroom windows, but there'd been a spate of break-ins, sliced window screens, the newspaper warning citizens not to trust nylon screens, and I studied my windows and decided I needed metal bars. I called Wyatt, who asked how Chet liked his work. "There's nothing more useless than a man without a job," Wyatt said.

I said, "That's true for all of us." Wyatt said, "Honey, he needs a job to raise him up. Women don't, not the same way." And I felt bad for Chet, who'd assumed that Wyatt had seen his own ambition mirrored in Chet, but Wyatt had seen need. Noblesse oblige, I thought, the obligation of those with higher rank to help the lowly. Day by day, I'd lost sight of how strange our life had become, Chet's aimlessness, our precarious finances. On the phone with Wyatt, I acquiesced, acting feminine, frail, saying I wanted to open my bedroom windows. He urged me to lock them and turn up the air conditioner. I couldn't afford that. I'd been counting on warm weather for savings because the coal furnace had cost a fortune. I said, "Please, I need fresh air." He said, "I'll send a man over."

The man, Hiram, was so old and unsteady as he got out of his truck I worried he couldn't carry his ladder. Slowly, he put quarter-inch mesh—fencing to keep out snakes and rodents—over my windows, with metal washers under the screw heads to keep the mesh from pulling loose. No one could break in now without using metal snips, Hiram pointed out. I handed him tools. I helped measure. I steadied his ladder. Hiram said, "You want just two windows done?" I said, "I can lock the other windows. I want to open these at night. I can't afford to run the air conditioner to cool off the wrong side of the house." Hiram said, "That air conditioner is as old as you are, girl. Used to belong to me."

I said that, as landlords go, Wyatt wasn't bad. Hiram frowned. "He's taken a shine to you then." Hiram was married to Wyatt's sister. She had dementia. "He and I are cordial," Hiram said, "but we don't see eye to eye. I've been a rabble-rousing union man since the thirties. But some strikers got shot. Union's been a hard sell here ever since."

I'd had menial jobs. Now I had a job with a future if I was assertive but not too assertive. I saw Sally watching out the window as Hiram and I went to the front porch, the wide-open one. Sally once dreamed she was wearing a waitress uniform as she cooked and cleaned, she'd told me, and she had a revelation: "Serving gives us power. It makes us needed." This had been the rationale for wives for at least forever. But once you tinker with so-called normative gender stereotypes, the established division of labor and rewards gets confusing. I was paying rent, utilities, the car note, credit cards, my student loans. Chet was making money but spending it, like the stockbroker's wife who shopped and called it work. Hiram sat down. "Are you management or labor?" he asked me.

A few weeks later, Hiram came back and fixed a door latch and put up a light with a motion sensor. "To make you feel safer coming home. To make you feel safer inside." I already felt safer in my caged bedroom, dimmer by day—gray mesh—but secure and breezy at night, a fan stirring the lace curtains. Hiram and I sat on the porch, eating Moravian cookies he'd brought me, sipping iced tea, and he talked about his brothers, three who'd worked in the mills, two who'd worked down in the mines, all dead now.

When Chet came home, he called Hiram my seventy-eight-year-old boyfriend. But Hiram was my friend, period. During the Depression, Hiram told me, the WPA had sent bookmobiles to the mills. "That's how I got to be a reader." He'd quit school at age fifteen. His brothers had too. He still read books from the library. He asked about my job.

I explained what it meant to be tenure-track. He said, "Probation. What you're saying is they got you on probation for now, girl. You got to look sharp." I nodded. It would take hard work and good luck for me to publish in time for tenure. I told Hiram that Chet coming home for the

summer—he wouldn't have new contract work until fall—was bad tim-
ing. Chet's TV, his two TVs, as I explained, echoed through the small
house. I'd shut the door to my study, but Chet had trouble letting me
write, coming in, for instance, to ask where we kept the SOS pads so he
could clean the backyard grill. Under the sink, I'd say, deep in the logic
of a paragraph that had nothing to do with SOS pads.

Chet wanted to use his last check to buy a truck for $1,800 to rebuild
its engine—to keep busy, he said. I'd admired old trucks. We needed
another vehicle. Yet we'd gotten by with one so far, and I thought we
should use the money to pay bills. But it was summer. Even though the
air conditioner was on high during the day, I worried Sally could hear
us argue. So Chet and I headed into the country to buy a sky-blue 1959
short bed Ford. Chet worked on the truck on the driveway a few feet
from my study, where I tapped away on my big computer. Sally, seven
months pregnant, admired Chet's handiwork. Ginna, selling Amway,
dropped by and said, "I admire a man who can do all that."

Hiram looked in on the project one day too. He was polite—visiting another man's wife. Yet he frowned as Chet changed his diction to
speak to Hiram. When Hiram arrived, Chet said, "Howdy." Then: "An
old truck is like a pig in a poke, hey." Hiram nodded, wary. Chet had
learned this countrified talk from summers he'd spent with his crazy
grandma and revived it for Georgia, where he bartered with farmers for power company easements for the lowest price. Down-home
talk helped farmers see Chet as one of them, Chet explained, not as a
smooth-talking city slicker. "That is smooth talk," I said. Chet said,
"It's my job to make the best deal. That's what business is."

When I tried to understand this marriage, broken but still running,
advice from my mother's era made the most sense: couples argue about
sex, children, and money. Chet and I didn't argue about sex, because
neither of us was interested in it with each other. We wanted children.
Yet you have to have sex to have them. You have to have money, I'd
think as I watched Chet skateboarding with Sally's children. He was
like a kid, not a father.

The arguments that heated up, then, were about money. Most couples will argue about money, I told myself. Lately, because he'd been gone so often, Chet and I argued over the phone. When he was home, he sometimes made feints as if to hit me. I ignored these—like a teenager's bad moods. But in the daytime, we both tried to keep the noise down. I quietly said how hard it was to pay bills. He quietly said, "We call that robbing Peter to pay Paul." So I robbed Peter to pay Paul because I believed in, if not happy endings, then ways forward I hadn't discovered yet. And if I disagreed with Chet that an old truck was an essential purchase, I was grateful he had an outside interest—outside my window.

He sometimes needed someone to hand him a tool. So he'd borrowed Sally's baby monitor and put the mother's half in my study and the baby's half by the truck, and he'd be under its engine and call my name. I'd stop working, go outside, hand him a tool. I made headway on my second book as I heard the musical tinkle of a dropped wrench falling on concrete, followed by Chet cussing, then my name: *Debra!* At the end of the summer, I had a hundred new pages and a truck to drive when Chet went back to work in Georgia.

One day when school hadn't started yet but the town was filling with students, I stepped outside just as the undergraduate, Kip, drove by. He rolled down his window and commented that I wasn't wearing my usual gray, black, or beige clothes. "Of course not. It's not winter," I said. I had on a lime-green miniskirt I'd bought on the cheap, a white T-shirt Ginna had decorated with daisy trim on the sleeve edges, and white Keds. I was trying to look local. Kip said, "Wear, wear those clothes so bright." He went on in this vein, mongrelized Dylan Thomas, as I opened my truck door. It was a handsome truck, stepside, with custom chrome and four on the floor. I liked driving it. I liked that people didn't expect me—an egghead, a professional woman—to be its driver. Kip asked for a ride.

We circled the neighborhood, and when I approached the last stop my foot on the brake pedal went all the way to the floor, but the truck didn't stop. I pumped and pumped until the brakes grabbed again. Kip said, "Not the best sort of auto malfunction, you know." I called Chet. He said, "An air bubble. It's worked its way through the line now."

He was right, it seemed. The brakes worked fine until, a few weeks later, I was driving, with Ginna in the passenger seat. She was hooked on a TV show, she said, *Unsolved Mysteries*. I said, "On PBS? A mystery, not gory?" She shook her head no. "It's unsolved murders in life." I was trying not to focus on crime this year. "Wouldn't it be better to watch something soothing?" I asked. She said, "I'm getting a burglar alarm. My ex is paying for it." The brakes went out again, and this time pumping them didn't bring them back quickly. We sped through a stoplight, drivers honking. Ginna started yelling, "Lordamighty." Then the brakes worked, and I drove Ginna home, her eyes wide. When she got out, she said, "It's a good thing your husband loves you, or I'd think he was out to get you." She giggled. "And you're right I need to stop watching that show."

I tried to phone Chet to tell him. He'd be home in a few days, because my father and stepmother were coming for a long weekend, arriving Thursday, leaving Monday. I didn't necessarily expect Chet to be in his motel, but I'd leave him a message. He wasn't registered; I'd misunderstood. I called his supervisor's office. The secretary answered. I'd spoken to her before, and she always called me by my husband's name. "How are things with you, Miz Crosswater?" I wasn't meant to answer truthfully, to say that bills were accruing, that our house was not so nice or big as the one in Utah yet certainly more peaceful with Chet working. But people had such emphatic Southern manners, even in small talk that's mere social duty, mere recognition of another human presence, that I sometimes felt tempted. I said I'd forgotten to ask Chet where he was working, and I needed to call him. She said, "Back in a jiffy." The next voice on the line was Chet's supervisor.

"Miz Crosswater, this is unpleasant to relay, but Chet's not in Georgia." Where was he then? I asked. Or something like that. I shouldn't have. Because the supervisor said, "It's unpleasant to relay that I have no idea. He's not working for me now." I said, "Did he ever?" Of course, the supervisor said. Chet just wasn't working now. He was scheduled to work—the supervisor checked his calendar—next Monday. "Thank you," I said.

Chet had left me, I thought. Another husband gone. As anyone married a second time knows, a second divorce seems both harder and easier. Easier because you realize how quickly the promise, the covenant, dissolves. Harder because you resist serialized failure.

I've always agreed with Maslow's hierarchy of needs, paraphrased here for modernity: soul problems vanish if your bank account is empty. I checked it. No more empty than usual. I'd sometimes get a few thousand extra dollars, money from the small press, or university grants, and I'd put the extra money on credit card balances—like floodwater, I thought, rising no matter how fast I dug trenches. But what would I tell my dad and stepmother as, husbandless, I drove them around in a truck with bad brakes? Then I realized that Chet had left me in my own car, the registration and promissory note in my name. But a few minutes before I was supposed to go meet my dad and his wife at the airport, Chet pulled into the driveway, smiling and waving, no clue I knew he'd been missing.

I had the drive to the airport to probe the mystery.

He blew up, panicked. I'd called his supervisor's office?

I said, "You gave me the number. I've called before. How was I to know this was different? Where were you?" He'd been camping, he said. He felt like a pent-up animal in Greensboro. He'd rented time on a fishing charter boat too, and he knew I'd object. "Like I'm on an allowance." I said, "You did this alone?" I pictured Chet with a mistress who fished. We were speeding to the airport. He said, "Yes." Then a line so familiar I once heard it in a movie: "That's my story, and I'm sticking to it." I never found out, and I never will, where Chet went. Maybe camping. Maybe gambling. One of Chet's brothers had a gambling jones. Another had just been arrested for soliciting a prostitute.

At the airport, Chet and I acted happy, greeting my dad and his wife. I felt like I had in the ER in Utah, this visit another crisis Chet and I would weather. In a relaxed moment, I told my dad and his wife that

Chet and I were on a tight budget—paying off expenses, Chet's work just picking up—and they were shocked because they'd thought that, after the rigmarole of a PhD, and a book award that had warranted a feature story in the *Salt Lake Tribune*, I'd be paid like a real doctor, not like Dr. Monroe, Department of English.

Sunday night at seven p.m., the big phone that was a fax machine rang, and Chet's supervisor asked to see Chet the next day in the office, a hundred miles south, and when Chet came home, he told me the supervisor had lectured Chet for putting the supervisor in a difficult position, and the supervisor wasn't interested in mitigating details like there wasn't another woman, just the peaceful ocean versus an ongoing marital squabble about how to spend money. Chet was fired. It was my fault, he said, for meddling. Then my sister phoned and said my dad had enjoyed the visit, Chet especially, but that I'd seemed tense.

Sally told us about someone who needed part-time help painting houses. Chet would come home, spattered, passive, and work on jigsaw puzzles, one of his TVs on nearby, a cable extender from RadioShack snaking across the floor. I told his mother by phone that he was painting houses, that he'd fixed the truck brakes and master cylinder. I'd helped, pressing and releasing the pedal as he'd yelled my name. "He's as handy as a pocket on a shirt," I said, a jaunty phrase I'd picked up from Ginna. Chet's mother went silent. Then she said, "He was the brightest of my boys. I expected more for him." The *My School Years* checklist for boys, I thought: Doctor, Banker, Fireman, Policeman, Farmer, Pilot. I thought of this list again as I sat on the porch with Hiram, who didn't have children, and he told me one of Wyatt's sons had never latched onto a job. "If you don't get something steady lined up in your thirties, you'll flounder for the rest of your life."

One Sunday, I was across town with the truck because the Subaru was full of Chet's office supplies from Georgia, also housepainter's gear, and I was buying bulk groceries.

As I neared the last stoplight, a four-lane intersecting with a six-lane, the stoplight was yellow, then red, and my brakes vanished—defunct, gone for good. I picked up speed as I flew past semitrucks like barges with their blaring horns, cars with bleating horns. I got to the other side, yanking the hand brake, turned into a Dunkin' Donuts parking lot, but I couldn't stop, donut customers jumping out of my way as I circled the building too fast, exited, and rolled down the street into a gas station and up onto a curb, into weeds and trash, just missing a Dumpster. I called Chet. I was leaving the truck here and wouldn't drive it again until a real mechanic fixed the brakes, I said. Chet was watching football, he said. I said: "You've lost your mind. Come get me right now." If a woman who's walked away from a truck listing on a curb, now half-sobbing into a phone, seems odd, like a gas station clerk might stare, no. I was in the low-rent part of town.

Hiram drove over with Chet, and they hitched our truck to Hiram's and towed it to a place called the Brake Guys. Hiram drove me there to pick it up and tried to pay the bill, $69. "No way," I said. Hiram smiled. I paid with a credit card. The owner said, "Thank you. You and your father have a nice day." Inexplicably, Hiram and I were familiar, fond, but we conveyed this in a veiled way, talking in generalities about life's changing demands.

Sally and I talked about cooking, housekeeping. But not often now, awkward since I saw her daily. She'd asked me to be the baby's godmother, and I felt I couldn't. I loved her baby. Or not him: all babies. I'd been groomed to be a mother, but this was a physical urge, to hold a baby, any baby, smell it, stare in its face. And I liked Sally's older children, their knock-knock jokes that didn't make sense, their anthropological take on adult customs, their frank conversation, no hidden agendas. But it wasn't my time for children. I had to launch Chet first, find him his place in the world. "Where will I be as he grows up?" I'd said. Sally said, "But you're one of my best friends. My kids love you."

I said I couldn't because I had to be at work on the day of the baby's christening. "A Sunday?" she'd said. We had an event on campus, I said, improvising. I had to go early to set up—a probable impossibility, a fiction that, according to Aristotle, is more believable than an improbable possibility. But I never wrote down the date, and I was reading on the private porch when Sally's minivan pulled up and her husband got out, her children did, and she did, carrying the baby in his white bunting. She peered through the dark screen, came to the porch door, handed me a church program. "Here," she said, hurt.

So it was Ginna who met the self I'd kept hidden. One day she asked how I was, and I told the truth. Pensive, she chewed her lip. She said, "I have the solution." She always did. Amway laundry booster. A burglar alarm. She'd recently heard weddings were a good place to meet eligible bachelors, so now she was finagling invitations to weddings. She said, "Move—you have bad geographical luck here. Some regions are bad for some people."

That wouldn't help with Chet, I said. She said, "Leave him." I said, "I need him to leave me." But I couldn't figure out where he'd go. Onto the streets, spending nights at a homeless shelter? I couldn't just throw him out. I'd talked to him about where he wanted to be. Texas, he'd said. But his stepfather had a rule about no grown children moving home, too many grown children, first of all, and a safety net makes people weak, he felt. This anti-incentive had worked for the stepfather's children. They'd also been raised by a different mother and had different genes—nurture and nature accounting for the fact that they got something steady lined up so as not to flounder, and Chet and his brothers never did. Ginna said, "Move. It'll shake him loose, either all the way loose, or he'll get out of his rut." The nomadic cure, I thought, moving as a release from unsolved problems.

I looked at the national job list. There'd been no ads for jobs in Texas when I'd finished my PhD. But this year I found two. I applied for both, and one in Mississippi too, because it looked interesting, another new life that beckoned. I flew to the national convention on the red-eye, did all three interviews in one day, and straight home on another red-eye. I had calls for campus interviews, but I only went to two in Texas, because, as Chet said, we wouldn't like Mississippi. I accepted a job in Texas in March. I hurried to campus to resign. My department chair was shocked. "But not mad?" I said, irrationally, panting from the brisk walk. I'd felt duplicitous, two-timing my job. He said, "No, saddened. I think I speak for many of us when I say I thought you'd succeed here."

So my stint in North Carolina ended.

Before I left, Hiram arrived to take me out to lunch, and I got in his truck and rode to K & W Cafeteria, where we slid trays on rails and ordered food. I worried about Hiram's tray as he walked to the table, his half-dozen different plates clinking, his wobbly glass of tea, which slid to one side, and the tray fell to the floor. Hiram bent down and tried to pick up the crockery shards, to swab spills, but a cafeteria employee got a mop and told him to load up another tray. I asked to carry it for him. Grim-faced, he said no and brought it carefully to the table. Because he was embarrassed, the conversation was stilted, partial. He died that summer. Wyatt phoned me in Texas. Hiram died in the middle of the day in a rocking chair on his porch. Wyatt said: "A peaceful end. I know he was your friend." He had been. That afternoon after we'd eaten at K & W Cafeteria, he brought me home and said, "Best of luck to you, girl. I will miss you."

Kip, the undergraduate, invited me to a going-away meal too. His roommate would be there, and my husband was invited. I couldn't possibly, I said. Kip said, "What? Who cares? You're moving. They can't fire you." So I went. Kip made hamburgers and his favorite childhood dishes. Frozen spinach baked with Hidden Valley Blue Cheese Dressing Dry Mix. Summer squash sprinkled with Butter Buds. Freezer pie made with a graham cracker crust filled with a Cool Whip and limeade concentrate. After dinner, Kip's roommate pulled out a bag of pot. He and Chet smoked. I did too. I hadn't since I'd written my master's thesis. Pot had either gotten stronger in the intervening years, I realized, or I'd lost my tolerance. The next forty-five minutes felt like hours, or like I'd taken LSD—Kip's face, his roommate's, Chet's, cartoonishly young. Then I felt fine, but dazed.

Kip's roommate went to a bar, and Chet went too. "You don't mind," Chet said, already out the door. Kip walked me home, carrying a bottle of gin, another bottle of tonic. We sat on the dark and private side of the porch, the screened-in porch. On the public side of the porch, the door to the living room was wide open so Kip and I could go in and wrangle ice cube trays if need be, and I remembered those nights in Utah when my mother and her boyfriend stayed up drinking and clinking, and Kip said I needed to get a divorce.

I told him he was nervy and impertinent.

He said, "True. But someone had to say so. It might as well be me."

Chet's manners that night had seemed lacking to me too. Chet had only coercive power, I thought, while I had reward power, so all Chet could do was balk, resist, disturb the peace. He'd lately started talking about staying in Greensboro after I moved, living in a garage that belonged to the guy who painted houses, and doing upcoming easement work. I wondered what else Kip had noticed. But I never did get to ask Kip, younger than me, raised by a mother younger than mine, what he knew and I didn't, because a bleeding, half-naked man dashed out of the night onto the other side of the porch and was banging on the front door frame. Kip and I froze, silent, in our cube of darkness.

The man glanced around, not seeing us, and walked inside.

I got up and went inside too, blinking in the light. The man had a cut on his chest, and he was wearing cut-offs too short for a man his age. My fear of crime was a figment from another life already. Or I was drunk. I stood in my living room, the half-packed boxes, bare walls. "What are you doing," I asked, "besides bleeding?" All of this would make sense the next morning when the local paper would report that the grocer's a few blocks away had been robbed by a man in a blue shirt, that a customer called the police, an altercation ensued, and the suspect got away, throwing his telltale blue shirt into shrubs. But I didn't know that when he said, "Lady, please. Call me a taxi." I pointed at the door and said, "Get out. If you do so politely, I might." I didn't have to, because he bolted.

Kip was standing next to me. "Did you not see that he had a gun in his back pocket?"

I was still holding my gin and tonic. I looked at Kip. "I didn't," I said.

"You'll be fine divorced," Kip said. "Really. What's the delay?"

Depredating Deer

I decided to be undomesticated. Wild. Not coupled up. Not celibate. *I never will marry nor be no man's wife.* How do I account for the dozen years I tried to live this way?

Categorically.

But, first, the lay of the land. I arrived in the sky-blue truck, its brakes stopping on a dime now, towing a trailer of my furniture from Garnett's store, more scratched and threadbare after another move. "Take everything. Whatever you don't bring you'll have to buy again," my mother had said when I was still packing in North Carolina, and she'd called from Arizona, where she lived then, our telephone-only era during which, if her husband wasn't home, she sounded like herself, thrifty, thoughtful. If he was, she hung up.

I got to my new habitat, a swath of abruptly rugged hills separating coastal farmland from high plains. The university sat atop steep crags, the San Marcos River winding below. The campus was in shambles. Its former glory—buildings like limestone castles; acres of hibiscus; stained glass murals; paths leading to secret courtyards; a round building accessible by way of a footbridge that spanned a pond with red lilies—was masked by scaffolding and cement trucks. At a party, a professor who'd drunk too much told me that, after a scrappy tom fell through a Styrofoam ceiling onto a secretary, the university had hired a specialist to relocate feral cats but not yet the bats in stairwells.

Not-drunk professors rushed to assure me that the university, recently and generously endowed, was on the upswing. Because it had previously been a normal school, it had a long history of female administrators—a boon, I'd realized as I listened to one offer me a salary thousands less than I'd been going broke on in North Carolina. I'd been raised to believe that asking for money was impolite. Perhaps the woman offering the salary had been too. She smiled, helpful. "I see by your facial expression that I'm not even close." I'd nodded, embarrassed. She offered thousands more. But I was in debt.

So I lived deep in cedars and live oaks in a cabin more cavelike than anywhere I'd lived. It had mud-colored walls and a grubby carpet I covered with area rugs, including the faux-Oriental with traces of tar, wedding present from wedding #1. I'd been warned to wear boots outside—rattlesnakes. Come winter, I'd use the woodstove. For now, a tiny air conditioner kept me cool during the day. At night, I'd wake, hearing footfalls on sere grass outside a window near my bed and think: Who's out there? Who turned on the floodlight? The moon shone down silvery. Deer cocked their heads at me, collegial.

My other companion was Sim. A man in the parking lot of the village grocery store had held up a sign, FREE DOG. "This'll be an asset whether you hunt or run cattle," the man said. "What about as a pet?" I asked. The man pushed his hat back. "Can't say."

Sim rode in the back of the blue truck until Chet arrived from North Carolina in the Subaru—to visit family, to see if I'd get back together. I was still paying the car note. The Subaru was registered to me. It got better mileage. But I resented giving up the truck because, as I'd come home from the high-elevation university town to the higher-elevation village, driving across the skyline in a sky-colored truck had made me happy. The University of Disrepair had a casual feel, so I'd be wearing a homemade black dress, or the lime-green miniskirt with a men's black T-shirt, black tights, black lace-up work boots. As I drove the hills in the squat Subaru, I didn't get the same euphoric surge. Sim liked the denlike space, though. In the passenger seat, taller than me, he'd sigh, let go of his hypervigilant scanning of the periphery for potential threats, and put his paw on my thigh.

Sim sat alert, erect, next to my chair as one day I phoned my dad to ask to borrow $400 because I needed new tires, and I'd cut up all the credit cards. I told my dad I was getting divorced, explaining that Chet was chronically insolvent, not just out of pocket due to my career, and that I was living lean until I paid off bills—a rationale for divorce and borrowed money my dad found irrefutable. "I won't charge you interest," he said. But he worried. "What about your children?" The ones I hadn't had. I didn't have spare money or brain-room to consider children. I needed $400. I thought about saying that I didn't need to marry to breed, but I couldn't be so blunt with my dad. I said, "I guess I could someday maybe adopt." This filled the blank in his vision for me. "Yes," he said, relieved.

Dating and mating, then.

Category 1. No damage, short delays.

Category 2. Longer delays. Obvious escape routes cut off.

Category 3. Small structures destroyed. Evacuation required.

Category 4. Hurricane party. Mesmerized, I drank too much. Battered structures likely.

The problem with this metaphor is that I wasn't stationary, waiting for landfall. I moved across landscapes too, for example the village near my house where a man followed me to the hardware store, then a gift shop that sold office supplies, then the post office, where he memorized my return address to show up at my door and recite a poem he'd written, its rhyme scheme dependent on words with -*tion* endings: *all my perspiration, due to love's vibration*. Stalker Behavior and Rural Courtship Norms, I thought. Wondering how to respond, I finally told him that, during the twentieth century, poetry had abandoned end rhymes as harsh, artificial. "You'll see internal rhymes," I said, "or slant rhymes." He looked confused. "*Heart* and *dark*," I said, "not *dark* and *bark*."

On campus? Single professors?

My former graduate school classmate from Utah who now hated her lonely job in South Carolina asked me this by phone. An art history professor, grizzled, a bit rotund, had introduced himself, bowing. He'd met me at convocation: new hires lined in a row onstage. No doubt, he was lonely. This was 1992. The Internet wasn't invented. Or it was, but for use by government scientists to send research results to labs. One day I thought I saw a motorcycle guy—black leather vest, keys clipped to a big chain. But he carried a briefcase. I asked a female colleague who he was. She said, "Angry young man figure."

She introduced us at a dinner at her house. I'll call him Felix. Felix arrived with a cooler full of Budweiser and set it in the dining room. She asked him to put it on the porch. Conversation stalled. Felix said, "The university is exclusionary." I was cutting my chicken. "This university," I said, "or all universities?" He frowned. "Both." Our hostess said, "Nonsense. Everyone's kind to you here." Everyone had been kind to me, I thought.

A university that lists its second and third most famous graduates as George Strait and Heloise with her Household Hints isn't elitist. And even our most famous graduate, Lyndon B. Johnson, first taught in a Spanish-speaking country school. But I knew what Felix meant. I said, "People whose parents and siblings went to college before them seem more comfortable—in class, handling the red tape. For them, college seems like a career path, not a long-shot detour." I spoke for myself, but Felix blushed, angry. As the cooler of Budweiser emptied, he lounged near me with his proud, fierce face and mood swings.

I dated Felix for almost a year, Category 2, obvious escape routes blocked.

I'd stop seeing him, but then I'd see him at work.

Or he'd show up in my driveway, and I'd rush outside to pull Sim off Felix's car, and conversation resumed. Sim, who weighed ninety pounds, let women onto the property, but he lunged at men, including my landlord, or lienholder now, because he'd sold me the house, using my previous months' rent paid as down payment. Meanwhile, I bought a book about raising dogs, yet so far hadn't been able to follow the first rule: to move Sim outside, establishing myself as alpha. Sim came inside, cool in the summer, snug and fortresslike in the winter with a roaring fire and wood on the porch stacked across windows, blocking light.

But I sent Sim back out one night when he came in with a bloody squirrel, dropped it, and snarled as if to attack me when I started to clean up. I kicked him off my bed for good one morning when I noticed him on his back next to me across the chenille bedspread, snoring, jowls quivering, his big head on the embroidered pillowslip.

You might love animals in a spiritual way—*They do not sweat and whine about their condition, / They do not lie awake in the dark and weep for their sins*—or in a fantasy way—birds tying ribbons, or helping you do chores, or leading you down the right path. But you have to draw the line somewhere, I thought one summer afternoon when I came home and saw wasps as big as hummingbirds flying in and out of an attic vent. I bought spray ("kills from long distances!") put on pants, boots, a long-sleeved shirt, gloves. The day was hot. One hundred and three, the thermometer said. I put a lace curtain over my head and sprayed and ran.

I was outside one day when a man in a pickup stopped, rolled down his window, and said that cutting weeds keeps snakes away. So I scythed, then bought a lawn mower. I planted flowers too. I'd read in the local paper that deer ate flowers, but you fight back by surrounding your flowers with mothballs, or human hair from a barber shop, or bars of soap.

Or you sprinkle your flowers with synthetic wolf urine from the hardware store. Or mist them with a spray called Not Tonight Deer. But Sim, an asset whether I hunted or ran cattle, patrolled my flowerbeds. So I kept planting, having discovered this urge to dig, sow, water, fertilize, wait for bloom. Nightfall, I'd walk to the river and swim by moonlight, my arms and legs pale in dark water. Sim stood guard on the bank, protecting me, I felt, but the book said no, claiming me. He nipped my heels, rushing me home.

In August, I had to go to a two-week conference. I boarded Sim with a man who used to raise minks in huge pens. "Honey, a dog like this is happier outside," the man said. "Might even calm him down," he added, because Sim, at the end of his leash, had lunged.

I drove to the university town to spend the night with Felix—his apartment was closer to the airport. Felix was teaching summer school, and he complained that Chekhov's "The Lady with the Dog" didn't depict the underclass. But Chekhov *was* the underclass, I said. Once he'd made money, he spent it on people who didn't have any. I loved the story, its ending, its last word, *beginning*, demonstrating that endings-as-resolutions are artificial, unlike life with its culminations that undo again, new problems arising.

Conversation with Felix was like sex with Felix, combative. But, having been Chet's wife, I hadn't had sex in years. I didn't see sex as a means to an end. I saw it as an end. I should have been forthcoming about that. Or I shouldn't have slept with someone from work. But there are lots of people most of us should never have slept with. After sex that night, I lay in Felix's bed, nervous about the trip, the important conference. *Go and be your best self*, my mother had whispered the night before I started kindergarten, I recalled. Felix felt restless, or neglected. He pushed me out of bed and onto the floor with his feet. I stood up and turned on the light. "What?" Hangdog, he smiled.

After the conference, Sim was happier outside. But my flowerbeds had been ravaged. It was late to reseed. I'd fallen in love fast. This is like taking drugs—short-term pleasure, long-term ruin. My usual way is to meet a man, pledge myself to him while feeling suspicious yet hopeful he might be The One with whom I'd belong in the paired-off world; or I'd feel pressure to take myself off the market, to ward off scary or implausible suitors. I'd been in love with James Stillman those fleet weeks when the wanting was mutual, neither of us weighing the other down, and during wee hours with Max, who, as a favor to me, gave monogamy a whirl. I hadn't wanted someone badly since.

Now this time the longing and remembering—*he said*, and *I said back*, and *he touched me like that*, and *our eyes met but no one saw*—went undeterred too long, due to the vacationlike setting of clapboard cottages, Adirondack chairs, the vernal wood we wandered while pointing at writers one or both of us had read but never hoped to meet, and our most serious decision of the day the restaurant at which we'd dine that night. The conference was renowned for its aphrodisiac mood. A classmate from Utah had seen my name on a poster and called to warn me. "The careerist and sexual currents run deep there."

Did he know this firsthand? No. He'd heard. Correctly, maybe. Cardboard bins in the laundry rooms held free condoms, the conference director announced during his first-night keynote address. This was when heterosexual people first started using condoms again. Promoting safe sex was the right thing to do, the conference director said. As was protesting apartheid. He mentioned this too. But I'd be laundering a pair of jeans or a summer dress because the weather was hot, cold, hot again, and someone would wander in, grab fistfuls of condoms, and I'd see him two hours later on a panel discussion.

Landon and I located each other early in the same way that, on my first day of school, a boy in a knitted red sweater and I located each other and walked hand in hand through manic recess. One night I drank too many of the complimentary cocktails, and Landon and I woke together in the morning. The sex was incredible, he said. Fully alert, I gave it another try. It was. The conversation was too, like a good class discussion, but not dog-eat-dog, as school so often seems, because this was talking, not debating, not one-upmanship, and it was mixed, too, with Landon's asides about how he liked what I said about John Berryman, or that I lived in the hills with snakes and deer, or the way my hair tangled in the humid summer air, or the dress I'd sewn, or how I kissed. Had one person ever liked all these different qualities of mine at the same time before? No. Just my homework. Just my housework. Or just how I was in bed, flesh-and-blood and wanton.

But all things must end. Autumn leaves must fall. That's what I thought, flying home, deplaning, driving from the airport, surveying my pillaged flowerbeds. What happens in Yalta stays in Yalta. In "The Lady with the Dog," Gurov went home to Moscow and should have forgotten Anna and resumed his life. But if he had, we wouldn't have a story.

All I hoped as I unlocked my door, thinking it would take me time to forget Landon, was that he'd need time to forget me too. Landon was tenured in another state, living with a woman in a refurbished Victorian with a fountain that babbled as he sat alone on the porch, contemplating Lucretius or James Agee, while she watched TV and drank. But my key was still in the lock when I heard my phone ring. He had a plan. He'd leave his girlfriend, and we'd see each other every Christmas, spring break, and all summer, when we'd write in the day and make love at night. I was skeptical, though one colleague in North Carolina had a wife who lived in Ohio. A professor in Utah was married to an opera singer in Germany. This career mixes badly with marriage, you see. Dreams get sacrificed.

Before we gave up on each other, Landon told his department chair that he'd met The One. Landon's department chair told Landon to stop running up the department phone bill, calling me. Landon left his girlfriend; he moved into a cheap apartment. Yet there were no blinds on its windows, and he was used to better quarters, so he crept home. He got a therapist who looked like Bonnie Raitt, with her red hair and cowboy boots, but she lost Landon's respect by saying, "Many people see the proverbial cliff and think about jumping, but you literally jumped." He explained that *literally* requires a real cliff.

One night, I dreamed I wore a brown dress that was once shabby chic but now was just shabby—a wash dress, my taskmaster grandmother used to say—and I was in a lecture hall with marble floors, and Landon, in a suit behind a podium, said the Southern Agrarian manifesto was doomed but seductive, and I nodded in agreement, but in the dream I was in the back of the hall, hunched over an oven with a can of Easy-Off, greasy streaks on my forearms as I scrubbed, while well-dressed hordes whispered that Landon was brilliant. But he couldn't hang window shades in an apartment. And why, you ask, didn't I feel bad about his wine-drinking girlfriend? I did. I'd turned into a version of my mother's nightmare, the Other Woman, or at least the other woman. I didn't sleep. Landon's longtime girlfriend probably didn't either, I thought, unhappy, wandering the dark.

Then it was Veterans Day, no postal delivery. No artful, well-edited letter today, I thought. I was grading papers. No spontaneous phone call either. Landon had moved home; he couldn't use that phone. He couldn't use his office phone either. But there'd likely be two or three letters tomorrow, I thought. I was steeling myself to write a stern one, saying this extension of summer love had lasted too long into winter. The phone rang.

A woman on the other end introduced herself, saying she'd found my number on the cover page of a forty-page manuscript—the first forty pages of my second book that a writer in the audience at the conference had asked me for after hearing me read. My reading had lasted ten minutes, but the writer had wanted more. Then he'd given my pages to his editor. She'd buy the whole book, she told me on the phone. I wasn't done yet, I said. I had maybe fifty pages left to write. She wanted the paperback rights to my first book too. She said, "If you don't have an agent, get one, because we're making a deal."

So I was writing, blocking out worry, quibbles, dread, when Landon's letters stopped. Silence arrived as a pile of mail I sifted through, searching for what wasn't there: a hand-addressed, creamy envelope with a postmark from the town of S——. My worrying ratcheted up. I got sick. I broke out in hives. For ten days I thought he'd died in a wreck and no one would tell me. Or he'd come to his senses and wouldn't say so, which was less alarming, yet cruel. No, he'd had a grand mal seizure. When he phoned at last, he said, "I know you worried." I said, "I was okay. But I thought you weren't."

He still wasn't, he said. A seizure causes months of lethargy. He broke up with me. This was for the best because my breakups, evasive, apologetic, lack clarity. I hung up, thinking it was helpful I had that book deadline because deadlines preempt regret. And Christmas was coming, a holiday I found difficult—I'd need temporary seasonal help.

Not Felix, I decided, who still called because I'd come back from the conference too distracted for long conversation. Like a high school girl, I'd told him we needed to take a break. I thought it was a short leap from "take a break" to "break up," and he'd know. But he wanted to bring me food his mother had sent on dry ice. He wanted to buy me a wristwatch. I wasn't hungry, I said. Also, "I don't need a wristwatch, but thank you."

I met a professor, born in France, teaching literature-in-translation at a tiny private college in a neighboring town, Seguin. At a party, he asked the host, married to a colleague in my department, to introduce us. He borrowed the host's car to visit me in my dark cabin— darker as the solstice approached—bearing wine. He told me I drank too fast. "Like a thirsty horse," he said. Yet I was not unattractive, he said. Could I drive him to the airport for his departure for his Christmas holidays because he didn't have a car, not because he couldn't drive, but because he was bad with money? "Hopeless," he said.

In mid-December, I met Jed Pharr in a village restaurant. He was tall. He had a huge beard and eyes that were blue or green, shining or sad. He owned the restaurant—the building, not the business. He owned a house next door. He built using nineteenth-century designs, insisting, for example, that the stately house next door, with star-shapes hanging like pendulums from its eaves, have an outdoor staircase, since settlers didn't waste interior space on stairs. So the house sat empty because no one wanted outdoor stairs.

When Jed stepped out of his indigo-colored stepside truck onto my driveway, Sim charged off the porch, teeth bared, and leapt for Jed's throat. Jed used one knee to block Sim. I apologized, put Sim on a chain. I said, "He doesn't get it that he's a dog and I'm not."

Jed Pharr drove me to the tops of tall hills, pointing at small towns nestled in distant valleys. An appealing restaurant here, he said. Good music in warm weather in a natural amphitheater over there. Our last stop was an ornate bridge over a creek, leading to nowhere—to a tiny lot with a cliff behind it. Jed owned the lot. One day, tired of his clients, he'd brought his crew here. He opened a thermos and poured us cups of coffee mixed with reposado tequila. "Poetry," he said, about the bridge. "Form. No practical function."

That wasn't his line. The editor of the small-town newspaper had written it.

It was a beautiful bridge.

For Christmas, Jed bought me a poinsettia and a bottle of tequila.

His eyes changed according to light, I realized. He was fifteen years older than me, not old enough to be my father; I was nobody's midlife crisis. He'd gone to college at the state's best school, but what he knew didn't sound familiar. Or all business majors have just a cursory acquaintance with history, philosophy, literature. I meant to date him briefly.

As a young man, he'd run one of the first catfish farms. He showed me a photo of this self—no beard, wearing a double-knit suit and a cowboy hat, on the House floor in Washington D.C., lobbying for catfish. He'd married and raised a child. He'd divorced, not amicably. He'd imported tequila. He owned an antique machine that made adobe bricks from straw and sand, because new adobe (concrete covered with painted stucco) offended him. He built houses for people he liked. He'd just bought property in a far off mercury mining ghost town filled with decamped-from-the-American-Dream former strivers, a wild west where men outnumbered women. On the way to visit this property, we stayed at a restored grand hotel in Marathon, Texas, where we ate roast quail, drank champagne, and slept in a room draped with Victorian fabric, train whistles waking us at night.

Then we went to the mercury mining ghost town to see Jed's abandoned dance hall made of real adobe. Its roof had blown off seventy years earlier. By day, the former dance hall felt like a container of light, its walls as bright as egg yolks, the turquoise sky, the homemade adobe

bar with art deco aspirations, curvaceous, geometric, and then the surrounding cell-like rooms that, we surmised, had once been whores'
bedrooms. Jed and I slept on a pallet on the dance floor, staring at mil-
lions of stars, one or two always falling.

When we bought ice at a place people called the Straight Store because it was run by fundamentalist Christians, I stayed close to Jed,
and Sim, who tolerated Jed now. Men who lived in cars or rusty trailers
crowded too near. I registered a doubt: Jed liked it here.

But Jed's assorted ventures sounded enterprising on a summer trip
he proposed we take to Spooner, Wisconsin, where, flashing a credit
card, he paid for every meal and talked to my dad, who owned the auto
parts store and, once, a tire shop and little gas station. They talked
about business, the suppliers, the employees, the customers, so necessary but annoying. Then they'd cheer each other up, pouring another
drink, and quote Dale Carnegie: "Take a chance! Life is chance!" When
my dad talked to me, he talked about weather in Texas, weather in Wisconsin. Then we left, Jed waving from his truck, and my father, stepmother, sister, brother, nieces and nephews, said goodbye, a chorus of
sighs, murmurs: Jed Pharr was a brick, a saint, a piece that would fit
the puzzle, me.

James Stillman weighed in too. In recurring, unsettling dreams,
he was dying. No deathbed. No last breath. A pair of low-order angels
wearing navy blue uniforms took him away in handcuffs. He'd whisper
to act as if I didn't know him. This was like a plan we'd had when I'd
slept at his house: if he got busted, I didn't know about the drugs. In
these dreams, arrested by Death, he told me to stay alive. But in a new
dream, he stood at the end of a hall I recognized, a hall with a green
phone, and said: "Better." James, forever young in ragged Levi's, said:
"Man, I'd be watching you with those other guys and think, damn, she
could do better. A little better this time." I woke, annoyed or pleased.

I used to split myself in two. Or I believed I'd split myself in two: a
bookish self; a homespun self. A third self had emerged: emergency.
I'd been having sex on and off for twenty years, but I'd been so intent

on being good in a one-time man's career, being good in a system of courtship where men pursue and women accept or demur, that I'd curbed the desire for what I'd had for a few hours with just a few lovers and never with a husband.

Or it's biological, animal fact. I was thirty-five. I didn't want to hope for sex to get good, better, best. I wanted it best now. It was. So I was three selves now. Jed suited two. My work self had survived alone so far, I thought. But lying in bed with Jed after luxuriant, frantic, slaking sex, during the pillow talk, I'd think how different this talk was from talk I'd had with Landon, though not for long—my conversations with Landon in tangled bedsheets lasting just ten days and ten nights, but countless hours by letter and phone. I'd talk about work *at* work, I decided, and not with Jed, who looked anxious if I did.

Fragmented thinking, I thought. Old vistas. New frontiers.

My wandering grandmother would run away from home, and people brought her back. Playing separate roles for separate spheres—roles that well-adjusted people keep inside "healthy boundaries," to use the lingo—isn't schizophrenia. But schizophrenia is statistically high among first- and second-generation immigrants, I'd recently read, among first-wave feminists too. It's a disease, of course, a breakdown of neurological function. But researchers speculate that, for those predisposed, the radical stress of dividing the self between one world and its rules and another world and its rules serves as trigger.

One night, pillow-talking, Jed told me about long ago losing his passport while buying wholesale tequila and spending four days in a Mexican jail. I asked how his wife had worried. He said, "She was still trying hard to understand me then. It was ten more years before she gave up." I asked if he'd tried to understand her back. He sighed. "At the time, no. It had to be hard, my plans changing hers. She'd weigh in, but I didn't listen."

Another night we lay curled in opposite directions, Jed's face upside down, so when he blinked, his gray-green eyes blinked from the bottom up. He looked like the movie character E.T., I told him. Jed's dad once saw a UFO while planting onions, Jed said, and Jed believed aliens had been here, still were. But he didn't believe in the moon landing.

"What?" I said. He was the first moon landing denier I'd heard of. It turns out that, according to a Gallup poll, 6 percent of Americans are moon landing deniers; 20 percent, if it's a Fox News poll. Jed turned defensive. "Why did we never go back there then?" I was pacing while wrapped in a bedsheet, upset, though I wasn't sure why yet. "Because Congress objected to the cost. Because the point of a race is the finish line. This is bad logic. Little green men mastered interplanetary space travel, but humans who can't get to a nearby celestial body convinced journalists to televise a hoax? Not to mention a problem with all conspiracy theories—hundreds of people won't keep a secret."

He got up and left, angry. He came back a day later. Did we break up because we disagreed about space travel? No. He never brought it up again. No, because we didn't always talk about concepts and hypotheticals. We talked about cooking, sleep, weather—weather so central to what linguists call phatic talk, talk that's all mood-calibration, not information. We talked about Sim, who attacked the workers I'd hired, because I'd used money from my book deal to gut the cabin, tearing out murky paneling and old carpet.

When we pulled out the carpet, so many years of dirt had sifted through, despite my three-times-a-week vacuuming, that when I first saw the slab I thought it was a dirt floor. It was a dirty floor. I sent workers away and swept. I got on my knees with a Shop-Vac. I was putting tile in every room, and painting cabinets, walls, outside walls, replacing the leaky roof. The cabin wouldn't get bigger, but it was going to be airy and light.

While I was turning my cabin into a tidy cottage, I got a phone call asking me to apply to be the director of a creative writing PhD program in a Great Plains state university, a good program with good students. I'd visited it, teaching a class, doing a Q&A. The current director had retired unexpectedly, the man on the phone said. The month was May, nowhere close to the time when departments interview, but the department had to fill the post quickly and well. I was their first choice.

They knew my work. I'd do the interview by conference call. I said, "No thank you. I've moved so much."

The man on the phone said. "We'll pay you more and reduce your teaching load. We'll pay your moving expenses too. Sleep on it. I'll call back. You're deciding too quickly."

Jed agreed. He beamed, finding this area in my life—besides tequila, day-trip destinations, and whether I wanted a tin or shingle roof—where he was expert. Eating carry-out food in my cabin that wasn't a cottage yet, he said, "You don't ever turn down job interviews that fall in your lap. If you get an offer, you tell your employer." This seemed like trying to make someone jealous, like asking for proof that I mattered. "No," Jed said. "It's establishing your genuine market value. Your employer will likely match the offer." If not? I asked. Jed said, "You stay as you are." But I'd have to take the job, I said. If I told someone I was thinking of leaving and someone said go ahead and leave, I couldn't stay, not with dignity. Jed shook his head no. "You're confusing work with love."

I cleared painters out of the house and did the conference call interview. The next day, I had an offer. I told the man on the phone I needed a week to decide. I made an appointment with the woman who'd first arranged my salary in Texas. I couldn't play it Jed's way, as sorely tempted, because she read my facial expressions well. I stared at the floor and said I hadn't been looking for a job, that I was remodeling my house and planning to stay, but this job offer came out of the blue. She finished the conversation for me. She said, "Naturally, we'd like to match the offer. How many days do we have to try?"

I was away at a conference in Pennsylvania, sleeping in a lumpy bed next to a phone, when I decided I had to take the new job. I pictured myself in a new state—with a bigger house, better groceries, a newer car. The phone rang. "We can match the offer," the woman administrator in Texas said. "We can't make you director of a PhD program, because we don't have one, but we'll match every other aspect." The mirage-vision of my new future stayed in place. I shook my head, willing it to go away. I conjured the limestone campus in Texas with it fiery flowers, my cottage soon to be airy and light. I shivered. Pennsylvania in June is chilly. I want to go home, I decided. I said, "Thank you."

Sim got bit by a rattlesnake, and the vet said to hold a compress on Sim's chest, and he might live. I'd once tried to clean a tiny leg wound, and Sim bit me, but now he laid his head in my lap like a hurt cowboy staring at the kind schoolmarm, and the wound drained. Afterward, he neglected deer patrol, so sometimes I chased away deer from my flowers.

Jed Pharr told me one morning after we'd drunk too much that he felt like he needed a PhD. "Why?" I was serving eggs, biscuits. He wasn't sure, he said, ornery. Yet he'd hated college, I thought. He'd complained about studying for a real estate exam. It seemed clear that, to paraphrase Shakespeare, my PhD was an impediment to the marriage of our whatevers. Minds. Bodies. Our love wasn't love if it altered while encountering alteration. My dad once said: "I don't see how anyone could have stayed married to you—starting with a waitress, ending with you now." Hence, I'd led a fitful life.

But movies started getting filmed in Texas, and, with Jed's knowledge of place, his carpentry, he was making a career swerve whether I objected or not, he said. Like I was the ex-wife, I realized, who'd disapproved of the tequila business, or the adobe business. The new job impressed people, life on the set: handing Tommy Lee Jones a cup of water with spray-on mist to make the cup look as if it had beads of condensation; searching junkyards for a radio to put inside a truck Kris Kristofferson would pretend to drive.

Jed would be gone for months, and I'd visit him for a weekend now and then. This left me more time to work. Reunited, we'd make love, then sleep in each other's arms. On one visit, Jed told me he'd paid for the grand hotel bill, the trip to Wisconsin, the bottles of wine and tequila, while not earning a red cent. I'd cooked for him or bought him clothes when his wore out. Not equal. "Why did you spend money you didn't have?" He said, "You'd never been anywhere for fun. How else would I date you?"

Complicit, I'd fallen in love with it all. His moody eyes, his lean body, the lovemaking, the whirlwind fun fun fun tour. I offered him money, but he was almost from another generation; he said no, emphatically. At least for now. He had that new job.

A movie was being filmed in a border town where Jed's family lived, including a brother who'd made a fortune building colonias—slumlike housing developments. I later realized that selling houses on land that won't have electricity or water for years, if ever, requires cozy relationships with corrupt judges. At the time I knew only that Jed's brother, Vick, paid the house note or rent for every relative except Jed and Jed's sister. But Vick had given Jed start-up money for all of Jed's businesses, Vick told me, shaking his head: "I never thought there'd be so many." Jed and I once stopped by Vick's house as Vick paid workmen to chase an owl. An owl near the house portended death, Vick explained.

No wonder Jed believed in conspiracies, I thought. Because Vick's wife was from Mexico, or wasn't. She was from Germany, she said with a Mexican-Spanish accent. Jed's sister was married to a rich rancher. She bought a house her husband didn't know about and filled it with furniture and Navajo blankets. She had a boyfriend everyone liked except that, unlike the husband, he wasn't rich. Jed's eighty-year-old mother had never been told her oldest son was dead. She thought he was living in a trailer park, drunk.

I didn't find this out all at once. It took the entire summer.

The production company would have paid for Jed's lodging, but Vick loaned Jed a little rental house for the length of the shoot—to make our weekends together pleasant, Vick told me as he met me at this house on the edge of a colonia, the former manager's quarters, to give me a key, telling me he'd had the house cleaned and filled with furniture. It was a burden, being naturally generous, he added. And Jed and I must keep the loan of the house quiet because Vick's wife would object. I thought Vick's wife would object that the house, loaned to Jed, wouldn't be earning rental money. I didn't yet know the extent of Vick's ill-gotten riches or that the secret about the house was me, not Jed.

It was summer. I wrote steadily, but every other weekend I drove to

the border town. Besides Jed, Jed's mother, and maybe Vick, everyone must have assumed I had my eye on the family fortune. Jed's sister—hoarder of Old West antiques and Talavera pottery—snubbed me.
Vick's wife and children did. I asked Jed why. He said, "Who cares?
What's that *hyper* word you use? Hyperanalytical. Don't be so hyperanalytical. What's the other word you use? Persona. You'll need a new
persona to get along down here."

But I couldn't help wondering. They thought I was too young for
Jed? I was somebody's midlife crisis? The only relative who smiled at
me was Jed's mother. I'd bring groceries and cook her dinner. I still
remember a photo Jed took and then enlarged because it made him
happy to see me in his mother's kitchenette, holding a saucepan as she
tied a polka-dot apron over my pretty dress, as she would call it, and
hugged me from behind.

Or I cooked at the house Vick provided—chicken baked with ol-
ives, capers, figs; cucumber salad; couscous; chilled wine. We'd invite the prop people, the makeup artist, the location scout. For a few
hours people who didn't write books, but they read them, sat on a
patio surrounded by a trellis that hid the steel fence with razor wire.
There'd always be a live band deep in the desert, playing conjunto. A
hot wind blew my cloth napkins off the table like tiny kites. My sun-
dress billowed. Sim sprawled on concrete. Our guests ate with gusto,
laughing. Jed said, "You have no idea how much thought goes into this.
Note red tomatoes on a yellow plate. Presentation increases appetite."
True, I loved to cook, combining my mother's home ec lore with all I'd
learned as a waitress, listening to chefs. Conversation flew, never once
touching down on the poverty on every side.

When Jed went back to work one Monday morning, I went into
town to say goodbye to his mother. She told me how, when she was a
new bride married to a sharecropper, he came home drunk, and she
locked him out. When he was halfway through a window, she slammed
it on his back. "Did he get mad?" I asked. "Oh no," she said. "He knew
better than to drink." Clear-cut conflict resolution, I thought. She had
the right to anger, nothing else. I said, "Was he hurt?" I never found

out because she answered her phone with the enlarged dial pad that blinked when the phone rang, and when she hung up she was upset. "You have to leave, dear. Vick's wife is coming with a relative you don't know." She even said "shoo" as she opened her door and shoved me through.

I didn't blame her, I thought, driving. She got flustered. "I'm a flibbertigibbet," she'd said once. She'd had Vick when she was sixteen, and now she lived on Vick's largesse, his wife's too. And who was the relative I didn't know? Jed's semi-estranged daughter? I sighed. Sim, in the passenger seat, sighed. He laid his head on my shoulder. Next, I saw flashing lights. I was being pulled over—the border patrol, looking for drug mules.

An officer with mirrored sunglasses asked for my license. He glanced at my overnight bag, a box of kitchenware, a laundry basket with bed linens I took to and from the bedroom in Vick's little house. Whore's bedroom, I thought. "One last question," the officer said. Sim hadn't moved his head next to my ear, but his growl amplified. The officer asked with a trace of a smile: "Are you both U.S. citizens?" Then he said, "Get back to civilization. If you run into trouble down here, your dog friend won't be much use."

Jed's mother started to die, and he moved in to oversee the home health care he didn't trust. When it was clear her dying would last more than a few weeks, he stayed, paid by Vick. I was focused on a new book coming out, the advance from it that would purchase a car, and an addition to my house if I kept it simple. "Extend the cottage motif throughout!" a colleague's wife said when I held a party in honor of another colleague's engagement.

I'd given up the wild life. I was moving on, forward. I wanted to be a mother. This can't be explained entirely rationally. I'd been raised to be a mother, yes. I'd never *not* hoped to be a mother. My wanting turned urgent now: biological, animal fact. I'd once been a child with my doll, Gisele, I thought. Then I'd gone on The Pill to delay my motherhood, not eliminate it. I'd married husband #1 with his lovechild a precursor to the child I'd one day have myself, I'd assumed. I'd married husband #2 because I'd wanted to be a mother, not *his* mother, though. Motherhood was one facet of traditional female identity I couldn't let go. I could forgo being a wife, I knew, but not being a mother. I thought hard about my decision because adoption requires months and months of interviews in which I'd describe why I hoped to be a mother and what kind I believed I'd be.

As I spoke to social workers, I realized I'd be a mother not so different from my own—until she got distracted by the end of one marriage, that is, and subsumed into the perpetual crisis of another. Given my history, marriage seemed like an obstacle to good childrearing, I thought, not an aid. Single and focused, I'd cook, clean, sew, nurture, set rules, and enforce them gently. I'd respect the ways my not-yet-arrived child would be different than me. I'd be just like my mother and her mother before her, but changed, a new rendition of an old recipe, an improvisation. I'd retain only the best bits of the past, modified.

I'd researched adoption using the Yellow Pages and the telephone because, while the Internet had been invented, the local dial-up server—run by two guys in a pole barn, eating potato chips whenever I stopped by to tell them it was down again—took forever to load pages. But the Internet was showing up in student stories in my graduate fiction class. I embarrassed myself once, commenting in class that it was unconvincing for lovers to meet, as two characters in a student story did, online. A student—not the blushing student who'd written the story—said, "Um. Debra. No. Not anymore. Wider selection."

Then my mother's husband died, heart attack, and she resurfaced, sleeping on the floor of my study for weeks at a time as I pored over blueprints I'd paid Jed to draw. She was like a mother-in-law, I thought—wanting to bake cookies or tell me how to do my laundry, and I called her Mom though I didn't know her, not anymore. One Sunday afternoon, she watched football with Jed Pharr, both of them joyfully shouting at the TV. She said later, "He's wonderful. Who could ask for anything more? And he loves his mother."

Blood loyalty. Even in-laws—apart from Vick's wife because of the ferocious way she watched over Vick's money—didn't merit it. I didn't. I didn't care now. I'd once loved Jed, but he wouldn't fit into my new life as a mother. My own mother would, if she'd stop praising my step-father, her revisionist history, and turn back into the mother I'd once known. Still, Jed wanted to talk to me on the phone every night. He wanted to have sex when he trusted home health care nurses to take over for a day or so. He said, "I get so much out of a little time with you, I can wait for weeks." I answered a few of his calls.

My add-on was finished, my cabin converted first to a cozy cottage, then to a commodious house, by the time my daughter arrived: six pounds of dreams-realized. I had sex with Jed Pharr a last few times, my attention fixed on the baby monitor on my dresser.

So ended Jed.

I loved my daughter first, most. Forever.

And if, throughout this book, I've emphasized my slow-breaking take on Jed's strange clan, or my family's mistaken but enthusiastic impression of him, or a neighbor's advice about husband #2, or a land-lady's advice about husband #1, all along I was tapping into scant collective wisdom. Had I lived in one spot forever, I'd have had the verbal equivalent of courtship letters of reference, people who'd have known my lover since he was a child. But I'd lived all over, and I'd lived by my wits, making choices by myself. If I turned out to be wrong, having based my decisions on who was locally available, on who suited my past if not my present or future, I alone was responsible, alone.

I saw Jed once more when my mother died. She was still young. Her dying lasted just thirty-six hours. She'd been in Oregon with a new husband—nice, as far as I could tell. I flew to the funeral and back, and then I had to catch up at work while caring for my baby. Jed came for a day to help. Help me how? I was grieving, busy. After he left, I was carrying my daughter in her car seat down a stone path in front of my house, and I passed a flowerbed planted for shade—purple beauty ber-ries, white caladiums—and a rattlesnake cooling on wet soil uncoiled, rattled. I hurried inside and called Jed. "How could I help you from here?" he said. I heard a TV, the volume turned low down. His mother's dying lasted ten years.

The snake was gone by the time I went back outside. I looked everywhere in my flowerbeds that were lush, but designed, monitored, with bars of soap tucked under a rosebush, mothballs mixed with pentas, cayenne pepper on the leaves of a passion flower vine—ideas I'd read about in the local paper, article after article about the growing deer population with no predators except humans, and none of us hunted, so the deer were starving, but not in my yard, I thought, as a doe slowly chewed impatiens. Deer salad, I thought.

My daughter's days ordered mine now, her ethereal breaths through the baby monitor that stayed green, serene, until it bleeped red when she woke, hungry, the tempo by which I slept. One night Sim stood outside my window, barking. He'd turned so tame he wanted me to get up and chase a possum off the porch for him so he could go back to sleep. I pushed at the possum with a broom, then wandered onto the sidewalk in my nightgown and looked at the sky and thought I saw a falling star, or a UFO. I looked again. A plane flew sensibly, explicably, across the heavens. Nothing startling and lucky would streak into my life without years of preparation, I'd learned. Not a career. Not a child. It had taken research, meetings, paperwork, to become a mother the nonbiological way.

I heard a crackle in the dark. I'd lived here eight years now, the longest I'd lived anywhere besides Spooner. Apart from wasps, or a rattlesnake in a cool flowerbed on a hot day, and another that bit Sim when he was still macho, wrangling with anything that moved, I'd lived in peace with animals. Except when I didn't. A male with a small rack on his head was bent over my vincas, which were deer-proof, according to the gardening book. I said this to him: "You're not even supposed to like those." All at once, I was surrounded by deer. A big buck. Four or five smaller deer. A doe I recognized because every spring she had a set of twins, the newest standing next to her now. The deer looked at each other, a deer communique, as in: why is the woman in a silver nightgown upset? Next, the doe stared into my eyes so long I thought I understood her. She had a herd. A herd helps. For a moment, I thought her eyes said that. Then she blinked and started chewing.

A Dress Rehearsal

I was taking in new information so fast that I thought in headlines. *Well-Adjusted Man Marries Oddball Recluse. Daughter Sees Transition as Tween Movie Plot. Fifteen-Year-Old Hates Eggs. Husband Reasonable on Every Subject Except Baseball.* My ten-year-old daughter, Marie, and I had moved to Austin, Texas, to live with my new husband and step-son, a communal life requiring synchronized schedules, preferences, quirks. But I'd lost the knack. Or I'd never had it. I'd lived in the rural hills for eighteen years: single, then a single mother. Before that, I'd lived with husband #1 and husband #2.

My new husband and I had dated for four years. I'll call him by his real name, Gary, because we're still married. The dos and don'ts for dating with children, for blending families (*puree, stir, knead*), are common knowledge, unlike thirty years earlier when divorce was a scandal never discussed with outsiders, and details about what's wrong with your ex were discussed only with your children, already privy, so my parents reasoned. Or they couldn't help themselves, stunned by the newfangled moral disaster, divorce.

I'd used a sitter for work; I was averse to using one for leisure. My job was filled with deadlines and responsibilities, also interesting talk, so I'd mostly deferred the desire for adult company. Single professors abounded, younger than me, usually female. I'd dated via matchmaking websites, ruling out men who smoked, took drugs, didn't have postgraduate education: specifications that yielded up short-lived fiascos, also a handful of MBAs. I'm not anti-MBA. But conversation, Stage One in Seduction for Grownups, didn't fly. And selecting dates online—a bit like shopping online, this feature looking good until, close up, it doesn't—magnified the problem of no one to serve as character reference.

"You're picky," my mother had said before she died, suggesting unattached men around town, the man who changed the oil in my car, the man who cleaned the chimney on my woodstove. True, I wanted a man who'd studied the history of humanity; who'd also, at some point, like me, worked menial jobs and therefore wouldn't think I was a savant on the wild side of a social class rift because I had; who knew that running a tidy, books-balanced household where my child came first was as important, or more, than my career.

One Friday night, after my daughter was asleep, I sat deciding whether to answer a dating website message from an artist recently relocated from Los Angeles, twenty years my senior, formerly famous, he seemed to be saying. Then I got a regular email from a friend of a friend of a friend. Gary and I were being fixed up. Or provided with each other's contact information so we could fail or succeed in private. He already knew more about me than I did about him because he'd used an Internet search engine to see my English Department website bio and photo. All I could find about him was a quote in a newspaper story in which he explained that an unconstitutional law had finally been overturned.

Gary's first email demonstrated a concise prose style, also manners. I answered. In a few days, he said he didn't want to rush me since I was a full-time single mother, while he was a shared-custody single father with more flexibility, but we could meet for lunch at a restaurant halfway between our houses. He's tall. I confess I like tall men. The conversation was so engrossing I was almost late meeting my daughter's bus as she came home from her first day of first grade. This was the dilemma. I'd gone to lunch because my semester wouldn't start for a week, but her school year had begun. Times like this were rare. One of my e-dates once said about a former girlfriend: "I don't like women with kids because—and maybe that's what it takes to be a single mother—they're rigid."

When I was home, I graded papers, or read for class, or wrote. I cleaned house, letting my daughter run her toy vacuum next to my real vacuum, or I explained what dusting was and that I'd rather she didn't dust the shelf displaying my grandmother's vases. I shopped. I cooked. I took care of flowerbeds as my daughter dug in her own tiny plot, planted with carrots and pansies. Saturday mornings, she had dance class. Saturday afternoons, kids' birthday parties: piñatas, roller skates, cake, chitchat with married mothers. Every Sunday, I drove Marie to the university town, and we spent the day at the playscape and then came home and started our week over again, the alarm set early.

Saturday night, we'd watch the TV connected to the old antenna that came with the house when it was a cabin. The TV got two stations, one of them PBS. Some parts of motherhood are once-in-a-lifetime. The first time your child smiles. The first time she reads. The first time she says something more charming or insightful than you could and—understanding anew that someone other than yourself is real, separate—you love her more. But motherhood is mind-numbing routine too, doing laundry while saying, "Whoa. Do not jump on the sofa because you could fall, not to mention the walls are shaking." PBS helps because you can hear, if not watch, a documentary while doing chores.

But that doesn't extenuate what I'm about to confess, self-medication, engrained habit. I was in deep before I knew it. I'd grown too attached to *The Lawrence Welk Show*, which first aired during my youth, but airs for eternity now on PBS on Saturday nights. I was nostalgic for days when my parents were married, affectionate, and our family watched as my dad said hard work had lifted Lawrence Welk out of a small town and made him successful, and I'd scowl, thinking: do Gail Farrell and Dick Dale, who are singing "One Toke over the Line,

Sweet Jesus," know it's not a religious song? My wandering grand-mother had seemed smitten, a Welk groupie. I watched every week. My Saturday nights matched my parents' and grandparents' decades ear-lier. The music was calming, restful.

When Gary suggested going out on a Saturday night, I hesitated. But I told myself to take a chance, get tired. He offered to pick me up and drive me home—three hours of driving, impractical, half that if I drove to the city instead. I'd liked the way he'd looked on our lunch date, in a white, starched dress shirt with faded jeans, and boots. Yet I didn't know how he'd dress for dinner at a good restaurant. I'd dated men who'd shown up for dates in shorts and T-shirts, and I'd be over-dressed in jeans and a tank top with stylish shoes. This time, I wore a floaty black sheath that, depending on accessories, was glitzy or casual. I drove to the city wearing a pair of beaded flip-flops, sleek sandals on the seat next to me. I'd wear the flip-flops, or say I'd worn them for driving and then change.

He was on the porch when I arrived. I put on the sleek sandals right away and stumbled, crossing the grass. I said, "I'm glad I'm here at long last." Too enthusiastic. I meant the opposite, glad to have got-ten a sitter, to have told Marie over and over she wouldn't miss me, to have fed her, answered her questions as I'd bathed, dressed, put on makeup, questions about mascara, lipstick, perfume. Then the long drive. I was already weary. I blurted, "I'm a little overexcited, you see. I'm usually home on Saturdays, watching PBS. Last night, I dreamed that when I knocked on your door Lawrence Welk answered."

In the dream, a younger, nattier version of Lawrence Welk had greeted me in a 1950s square-shouldered suit. I'd felt pleased he was familiar but troubled he was old-fashioned, although we were the same age. I also thought: he's dead, right? I was going to a lot of trouble to date a stranger, I thought, yet I reminded myself to be open-minded, not superficial. Gary smiled. "I suppose I'm flattered. You blew off Lawrence Welk for me."

My plan not to introduce Marie to Gary ended fast. I came home from a fourth date in Austin, where I'd spent the night. Marie had spent the night at a friend's, with a family I knew well, I'd thought. When I went to pick her up, Marie and her friend, age six, and a brother named Brother, age four, were running down the driveway, almost to the highway, with backpacks on, leaving on a trip, they said. I drove them back to the house, where the mother and father slept so hard I pounded on the bedroom door to wake them.

Even without this unsettling morning-after, I'd hit my limit about how often I could be away from home. A month later, as Marie slept, I folded laundry while Gary watched baseball. He said, "I need to tell you something. I wasn't quite honest when we first met." I thought: my God, he has an STD, or he's addicted to crack cocaine, what? He said, "I exaggerated when I said I would never marry again. I would, if I keep feeling the way I feel now." I smiled and kept folding laundry. The next years passed easily except for the rationed privacy, so little time to talk, Marie always nearby; Gary's son, Fraiser, often nearby; not to mention the people from Gary's long roster of character references.

On holidays we went to parties with Gary's ex-wife and ex-in-laws, where we picked up Fraiser to take him to celebrations on Gary's side of the family. I'd stopped flying to Wisconsin for Christmas—Spooner so far from an airport, and we'd get snowed into Minneapolis, stuck in overheated hotel rooms, no toys or snacks, watching the Cartoon Network. I'd done my best celebrating at home with Marie and a tree, as Marie, indoctrinated, had pointed out that we lacked a dad and grandma. We didn't, if we spent Christmas with Gary's ex-wife, where Gary's ex-mother-in-law, with her thick Mississippi accent, urged Marie to call her Nana Pat. All the ex-everyones, including Gary's ex-wife and her partner, his ex-sisters-in-law and their partners, his ex-niece and children, bought Marie gifts. Nana Pat treated me like family too, saying, "My stars, I love Gary. I'd prefer him married to my daughter, but if it has to be someone else, you're nice."

Then we went to a small town due east of Austin, La Grange, where

Gary's parents doted on their grandson but seemed as if they'd waited years for a girl to visit them in her colorful dresses, chattering, bringing crayon-colored cards, offering to demonstrate her dance-class routine. I met Aunt Alvina, Aunt Gladys, neighbors. All attested, approved. Gary was a good man. The reputable lineage stories covered eighty years.

Harvest parties in bottomland. A grandfather who, when Gary was little, held Gary by his feet to see cotton entering the gin. Aunt Alvina told me about a time she went to a dance in a borrowed tulle dress. "Ach," she said, laughing. "I thought I was beautiful. But Texas in midsummer. I started to sweat after one dance. Dye ran in streams down my arms. I wasn't beautiful then." And they didn't like just anyone. Aunt Gladys told me to keep an eye on Zea, who came in to buy groceries and cook for Gary's parents, who were growing more feeble, confused. I felt bad for Zea. Outsider, I thought, no one to defend her.

Everyone inquired kindly after my family, then looked mystified. They'd heard of Wisconsin. But they'd settled in this area 150 years ago—except for the years when Gary's parents followed oil field work before returning to the ancestral county.

Gary's family knew I was a professor, but they'd have been as happy if I'd been a secretary. The University of Disrepair, on the upswing for years, is the most beautiful campus in the state now, an emerging research institute. This is a good time to call it by its real name, its sixth: Texas State University. Why had it had more names than a woman who'd divorced too often? At the turn of the other century, the not-recent turn, it was Southwest Texas Normal School, when *Southwest* was meant to describe a region in the United States. *Normal* was traded for *Teachers*, *College* for *University*, and so on. *Southwest* next to *Texas* got dropped since southwest Texas is four hundred miles away, not here.

Gary had watched the University of Disrepair convert itself from a local curiosity into something respectable. Like me, I thought. Yet I was guarded, discussing my own past.

I'd summarized it, bare bones. My first husband was a musician, never a good idea. My second husband had a temper. I'd been single twelve years before I met Gary, really? I mentioned Jed, and one dating website fiasco, a man with whom the short-lived romance had run its course, but he'd been fired, and I thought we'd mete out bad news and break up after he found a job and a small surgery I'd scheduled was over. He broke up with me over the phone. "Your surgery?" Gary asked. Botched. I didn't say that. Or that I'd asked acquaintances for help, awkward. Or that home alone, I'd had complications. I said that when I was getting my master's degree I'd inadvertently heard a professor describe me as "reasonably intelligent, but with unaccountably bad taste in men."

Gary looked worried.

When my dad came for a visit, Gary's office was in the midst of a big project. Gary drove out for a hurried dinner: hello, goodbye. My dad respected that Gary, a man, was busy. And I was glad that Gary missed my dad rehashing what was wrong with my mom, whom my dad had divorced twenty-five years earlier, and she was dead, which made the criticism sound more wrong, as my stepmother seemed to think too, knitting, repressing hysteria, a squeal, as my dad poured out half of his can of Pepsi and added booze, and it was hard to keep track of how much he'd had until he was staggering and scrappy.

Describing my past to Gary, I'd simplified because—according to the codes of my childhood—I'd lived like a man. Free love, the so-called sexual revolution, had its inconsistencies. After casual sex was pro forma, women who said No were unhip, frigid. At the same time, they weren't supposed to pile up a "number," the new term for copious notches on the bedpost that men are improved by having. I hadn't meant to be "a sexual adventuress," as I've heard Edna St. Vincent Millay and Martha Gellhorn described, which doesn't seem fair. Martha Gellhorn once said, pithy, that she'd heard male desire described as so urgent and primal that saying No had seemed as cruel as withholding bread.

The conventional wisdom would be that I'd been naive: wanting it all. Freedom plus routine. Go-for-broke ambition plus a home life. But I hadn't premeditated any of my wanting. I wasn't even ambitious.

I wasn't a pioneer either, a first-wave feminist—just a particle in that mass wave of women entering what had been, a generation earlier, a male province. Since first grade, I couldn't stop reading. And because my relationships had failed, or because I'd had to earn my way—which, in my mother's era, were one and the same problem—I'd stayed in school, no reason to stop. Age-appropriate and career-minded men, my equals, yet raised by homemakers married to breadwinners, had been as confused.

I didn't have to ask Gary the same questions because no one was a skeleton in his closet, least of all one of his previous selves. He came from a small town where higher education was rare, but no one was alarmed when a boy precociously interested in books bettered himself through school. Precociously distracted by books, I'd been expected to better myself by becoming an asset to a go-getting man. This time I could be, maybe, because Gary and I had met later in life and didn't have to decide where to live for whose career.

Our small wedding was in my yard. Sim, who'd lived to a good old age, had died peacefully under the porch swing. So I spent the morning before the wedding chasing deer while wearing an old dress and fancy hair—I'd paid a woman at a salon to pile it on my head and shellac it with spray. In the end, I augmented my ransacked flowerbeds with fake flowers from the Dollar Store, a trick I'd learned from visiting movie sets. It was going to be so hot, so uncomfortable, our vows so brief before people hurried inside to eat and drink in the air-conditioning, that no one would notice a few blooms weren't real.

Then I moved into the big, remodeled house in the city. A month later, we went to a party, celebrating Gary's semi-retirement after decades of service, and a few younger, female lawyers assessed me as future sisters-in-law might: was I suitable? Others lawyers regaled me with stories about how instrumental Gary was, how fun, how considerate.

I was wearing a dress and heels, and Marie was turned out in pink. My stepson, Fraiser, stood by, mature, serious. I'd stepped into the part for which I'd been trained, and my advanced degree was a helpful flourish. Everyone seemed startled, yet not exactly unpleasantly, that the books I wrote weren't typically academic: not quite this or that about gender in the twentieth century, not quite this or that about social class in postindustrial America. When we got home, Gary asked what so-and-so or so-and-so and I had talked about. I couldn't keep names straight. Gary seemed too casually curious, as if he worried I'd said something confessional, not lawyerly and close-to-the-vest, not the trifling small talk I'd spent my writing career bypassing, going instead straight for the secret, emotional core. I also realized I'd smiled nonstop while clenching my teeth. I was playing a role: last self. This isn't to say I didn't mean it. I was acting, and I meant it.

The children must feel the strain too, I thought. Yet, since Marie was little, she'd said I should find a dad. I read her entries in her English class journal: about a great brother, a great father. Her teacher said, "She's made friends so quickly. It's not easy in this neighborhood where most kids have known each other since they were babies. Their mothers likely met in Lamaze class." One day, when Gary said that I'd put too many doilies in the living room, that it looked like my old house, undeniably froufrou, both a home and a quirky domestic museum, I said, "Two is too many, then? I've winnowed. I'm down at least fifteen doilies." Gary had vetoed lace curtains. Fraiser said, "But I think it looks homey now." He asked for a few of my chairs and lamps for his bedroom. When I passed his open door I felt a jolt, a reminder that the past isn't gone, just off to the side.

But I was accustomed to small towns, not cities. The talk is different. Traffic is. Entering conversations seemed like edging forward on one of those ramps leading to the six-lane highway I took to work now. In reality, as in this analogy, my driver's ed took place on country roads known for blind spots and wild animals but little traffic. I spoke carefully to strangers. One day, I hurried to pick up my daughter at school. The mothers I met—ones who weren't clocked in somewhere until five-thirty—never hurried. I said, panting, because I'd run: "Wow. Parenting is labor-intensive, you know?" Two mothers made disapproving eye contact. One said, "I knew when I had my children that it's a huge commitment." A third mother said, "I think she's being funny. Did you have a busy day?"

I chatted with my colleagues at work, an hour away. I spoke on the phone to long-distance friends. I told happy news. This is key. The life you describe is the one you get. Yet I had niggling unease. I mentioned this to my husband. Maybe I was just confused, I said. "Maybe I'm not alone enough to understand what I think." He looked alarmed. Was I unhappy? Not that, I reassured him. I wasn't feeling myself yet. What self? Even if I was unhappy, we were married with children now. We didn't have time for existential quibbles. We got a call that Gary's parents were in trouble and needed help.

Aunt Gladys had gone to check. My mother-in-law had fallen. My father-in-law couldn't lift her. Irrationally, she wouldn't let him call the ambulance. Or rationally, knowing she'd end up in a hospital, then a skilled nursing facility, which is what used to be called a nursing home. For days, they'd camped on the floor, eating whatever food my father-in-law could put together and carry. "But where was Zea?" I asked. Gary said, "Maybe she asked for the week off. I'm not going to judge before I get her side of the story."

Her side of the story had gaps in it.

Knowing Gary would be the one to decide if Zea would keep her job when my mother-in-law recovered, Zea bought Gary a wrapped, be-ribboned gift, which turned out to be four crucifixes: a big, iron one for Gary; a big, calico one for me; a small, terra cotta one for my step-son; a small, polka-dot one for my daughter. And Zea had tried to make folksy conversation by saying, about Barack Obama, that she didn't mind blacks if they weren't lazy. She'd heard through the grapevine that Gary had married a woman with a daughter. And I still love Gary's family profoundly as I consider that not one of his relatives, raised in the South during Jim Crow, had felt the need to mention that Marie is black.

You, Reader, might think it's odd I haven't mentioned it, as if, as Marie's mother, I haven't adequately considered race and racism. In fact, I could write a book about what it's like to be her mother considering race and racism; I did write that book, my fifth, and this isn't it. What that subject is now—now that Marie's growing up and navigating her own shoals—is her business, not ours. At any rate, Gary told Zea that his parents wouldn't need her now. Aunt Gladys said, "People don't think Zea is—how do I say this?—good."

My mother-in-law languished months in the hospital, then in a nearby nursing home, befuddled every night at dusk. There's a term for this, sundowner's syndrome. Away from the familiar as darkness encroaches, the patient panics. Gary had been reconsidering my in-laws' house, its size, its disarray. No doctor will venture to say when he or she thinks it will be time for your elderly parent to go home—until the doctor does say, and then it's in two days. Quickly, Gary finessed the details of a contract for an assisted living facility in Austin. I made a list of furnishings from my in-laws' house to be put in the pickup and moved. Aunt Gladys packed clothes. I took over the shopping list from the facility: three sets of bed sheets, ten towels, hampers, a plastic cabinet with drawers.

One Sunday night in winter, Gary and I moved the furniture into a tiny, modern apartment. We whispered as we put together the bed, carried the recliners, set up the TV. It was after eleven when—and I felt bad for the old people asleep in the next room—I tried to quietly hammer mounts on the wall to hang a domed picture of Gary's great-grandparents and my mother-in-law's favorite picture of sunflowers. I hammered again, hanging rods for curtains I'd bought, unpackaged, ironed. Gary and I argued in whispers. Only the bed, chairs, and TV mattered, he insisted. Curtains and familiar pictures matter, I said.

Sunrise. Sunset. One each. My mother-in-law fell down within a day.

She was hospitalized again. Then another nursing home. Months.

Gary spent so much time in these settings, he started to talk about when our time would come. He talked about our house being our last with stairs. He dreamed he was trying to land an airplane, he said, but didn't know how and a crash was imminent. When I pointed out that this was a death dream, he said he didn't put stock in that abracadabra idea that, as you sleep, dreams explore pressing problems with day-time censors turned off.

His mother settled at last in a skilled nursing wing at the assisted living place. My father-in-law could see her daily, and it was cheery, at least the bird cages and fish tanks. The residents, not so much. Some reached for my daughter and stepson, wanting them. Or, mouths agape, slumped in chairs, eyes gummy and hazed, they wanted to be my daughter and stepson. "Gutta," one woman said, gibberish, or some odd bit of Czech or German.

Gary's mother never forgot who anyone was. But in the midst of talk about what we might do for lunch that day, she'd say she was using the time to go speak to Gary's teacher in the one-room school in Kirbyville because that teacher wasn't worth salt. Her memory served up long ago days in the same way that Gary's parents' house had as he'd dismantled it. He'd found a postcard from Aunt Gladys, mailed from Mexico in 1944. A jewelry box from Woolworth's holding a dog collar, and inside its lid, lined with fake satin, the name of a long-dead pet, the day it died, written in pen by my mother-in-law.

My mother-in-law started to die. We should call hospice, the doctor said, and a funeral director. The funeral director asked for the dress my mother-in-law would be buried in. She didn't have dresses. Her new clothes, which I'd bought for Christmas or Mother's Day, were velour warm-up suits with fancy zippers. I worried about clothes for the children too. My stepson found a pinstripe suit and red satin tie at a thrift store. I took Marie to a mall, where I also shopped for my mother-in-law's burial dress, without success.

I searched online. Prim, yet springlike, Aunt Gladys stipulated. Given these parameters, JCPenney was too hip. Did Montgomery Ward still exist? Gary stood behind me as I logged on. We scanned pages of women's clothes, tiny thumbnail photos. We paused, looking at one photo of "Watercolor Floral Dress with Daisy-Trim Jacket" right next to "Intimate Memories," a strapless minidress with holes for breasts to poke through and a black rectangle covering the model's nipples, though not her serene, catalog-model face. We searched and found more prim, springlike dresses next to peekaboo corsets and garter belts. "Is this website hacked?" I wondered. Gary said, "Or Montgomery Ward is trying to stay in business by covering every market niche, and they need a new website design." We ordered the "Watercolor Floral Dress with Daisy-Trim Jacket."

I'd planned three weddings. No funerals. I called a florist. The florist suggested two big bouquets, a big coffin spray, a corsage. I asked who would wear the corsage, and the florist said, "Any of the bereaved could. Or you put it on the deceased." I declined the corsage. I thought it would look fussy and wrong on my mother-in-law's Daisy-Trim Jacket.

Then she wasn't dying. We sent hospice away.

I was at a nearby literary festival that takes place on a tract of land with a restored opera house and nature trails—not that I saw these, because I was there a few hours when I got a text message from Gary. "She's gone. Dad and I just happened to be with her. Don't leave. I'll take care of the next phase." Marie was roller-skating. Fraiser was on a date. Gary texted both of them. "Grandma's gone. Don't worry. Love." He told me later that both had texted him back sad-face emoticons, which might seem to lack solemnity, but this was their first death, they did feel sad, and texting is the family lingua franca.

I talked to the festival director about leaving. Yet I should stay and honor my commitments, Gary said by phone. We'd had that trial run, everything set. It wasn't as if my own mother had died, I thought, or as if I'd known my mother-in-law for years. I felt I didn't have a right to grief, or to condolences arriving from strangers at the festival, and I'd answer that I was a newlywed, though middle-aged, but my husband was sad, and people looked confused. Was I coldhearted? Gary would be seeing the funeral director in the morning, finalizing plans. The festival was forty miles from the funeral home. I started worrying that Gary didn't want me there because he thought I'd say something peculiar. I know I'm a little strange because of the decades spent alone even while with others.

That night at the festival, awake in my cottage, freezing though it was spring, I thought about my mother's funeral in Oregon, where, because I was used to public speaking, I was asked to deliver the eulogy. Delivering my mother's eulogy was like teaching during the earliest weeks of the semester in that I didn't know the audience—the family my mother had married into—and couldn't say everything I knew, just what the audience could handle. At some point, my mother had converted to Catholicism. When I was little, she'd been so wary of Catholicism she wouldn't let me spend the night with a Catholic friend, worried I'd end up at Mass, spirited away. After her funeral, I went home. I was grieving the death of the mother I'd grown up with, not the one I barely knew who'd married again and died, though the new one had seemed lovely too. I said to my doctor, seeing him for other problems, "I haven't slept for weeks. My mother died suddenly."

The doctor had said, "Interesting. Not that I doubt you. It's just that most people would have a psychotic break." I'd had insomnia since I was a girl, daydreaming into night about Rapunzel or *The Secret Garden*, and I said, "If I would, I sure would have by now."

I stayed awake all night at the festival too, and in the morning I called Gary and said I was coming. I got in my car and drove back roads to meet him at the funeral home, where he'd driven over with the "Watercolor Floral Dress with Daisy-Trim Jacket." I told the funeral director that the florist had our order. Gary asked me to pick out the coffin. We wandered past brown coffins, white coffins, mauve coffins. He held my hand. I couldn't tell if he needed comfort, or if he was offering comfort, or if he was holding on in case he'd need to squeeze my hand to stop me from volunteering something he'd rather I didn't. Imposter syndrome, I thought. Why had I thought I'd ever be a good-fit wife?

By the day of the funeral, my husband's office was at the busiest point of the season. I was in the middle of finals. But we were ready for, first, the viewing, where my confusion about who wears a corsage led to an altercation. I whispered to strangers, thanking them for coming. "I'm Gary's wife." If the person still looked confused, I'd say, "The daughter-in-law." The funeral director handed me a corsage. I said I hadn't ordered it. He said, "But it came with your order. You may as well use it." I didn't put it on my mother-in-law. I decided to give it to Aunt Gladys. It didn't seem right to say: "The florist messed up, and I have a corsage lying around." I said, "Here's a corsage for you."

A white lie, half-true. No malice.

But Gary, who should have been a judge, pointed out later that even white lies cause trouble. Aunt Gladys's eyes filled with tears, and she thanked me. This was the death of her only sister. A few minutes later, a woman rushed in, hurried to the coffin, looked around. I said, "Thank you for coming. I'm Gary's wife." Marie was next to me. Gary was across the room. The woman said she was Zea. Then she said: "What have you done with it? Where is my corsage?" Confused, I stared at Zea's empty lapel. Zea said, "I ordered it for her in the coffin." Then I understood. I said, "It seems I made a mistake."

I wondered if I could ask Aunt Gladys to give hers back. Or should I try to order a replacement corsage? I was also thinking about Aunt Gladys, who'd been single her whole life, now living in her home-town, and Zea, divorced in a furtive way—how they'd turned out differ-ent. Aunt Gladys belonged to us, to others. Zea belonged to no one. I could have become Zea, I thought, not unsympathetic. Zea hit me. She missed my face. She hit my arm. I wasn't hurt. I was embarrassed. Zea left, hissing that I wasn't family, not really.

Before the service started, we waited in the choir loft. Then—a fu-neral is like a wedding—the relatives would be seated last. Men don't dress up for church here, I noted. Gary's male cousins, farmers, weld-ers, well diggers, wore jeans and western shirts. One wore bib overalls. He didn't have front teeth, but he smiled wide and kind at me, at Ma-rie hugging me, at Fraiser standing to the side, anxious. The pews were full. My funeral won't be so full, I thought. I'd lived too many places and lost track of too many people. My mother's funeral had been crowded, but the squadrons of attendees had belonged to the groom's side. My mother had been so recently married that it was impossible not to make that distinction. Moving and three marriages had scat-tered her friends.

A Dress Rehearsal

People trailed into my mother-in-law's funeral, including Aunt Alvina, whose quilting circle had made the food: kolaches, not unlike my grandmother's kuchen; trays of homemade sausage; pimento-cheese sandwiches, crusts removed. Gary's ex-in-laws came too, the ex-everyones and their partners showing support, some dressed like Gary's male cousins, because Gary's ex-sisters-in-law are gay. Nana Pat often remarks on this: "Can you believe it, Debra, that I raised not one but two gay daughters? But they're so nice."

Then the funeral director waited as we said that necessary goodbye before the coffin lid closes—necessary so you understand that death is death, not relocation. After the service, we drove to the cemetery. A historic drought was underway. Wind like a furnace blast blew across withered cornfields, and the striped canopy over the gravesite tilted, wobbled. I thought about my grandmothers' funerals, one in autumn, one in winter, colder, but the same incessant gusting. The faces all around me, austere and creased, saying prayers with German accents, seemed familiar. Done. We went to our cars.

Two weeks later, Aunt Alvina died. She was my father-in-law's sister. She had scads of children, so we didn't arrange her funeral, which was in a town near La Grange. Her funeral was bigger than my mother-in-law's. A table displayed agricultural extension plaques honoring her and trophies from the county fair. She'd been an exemplary cook, a seamstress, a driver of tractors. My father-in-law sat crumpled, stricken. Afterward, Gary drove him to the assisted living, and I left with Marie and Fraiser. Fraiser liked English classes best, and he asked me about the origins of modernism, and I was doing my best to answer—mass migration, the anonymity of a postagrarian life creating new freedom in terms of one's inherited identity, but also new loneliness—when I saw a familiar driveway, a long and winding approach.

I'm not saying that the name of the town where we went to Aunt Alvina's funeral hadn't rung a bell. When we used to visit Gary's parents, we'd go to nearby towns for dinner, and I'd been here before, in this east Texas town where long ago I'd spent a grim Christmas at a hunting camp not yet converted to a house, with my second husband, Chet, my father-in-law and mother-in-law #2, the broken furnace, crazy grandma, snoring in-laws. Everyone has a past, I'd think, as Gary drove us into town, and we parked next to a restaurant. But I hadn't seen this driveway in over twenty years. Curious, I wanted to turn down it, memory lane. But no telling who I'd meet, I thought. Myself, outmoded. I kept on driving.

My semester ended. I'd go to a professional conference in early July. Then I'd have a small surgery to repair damage from my previous surgery. The previous surgery had been exploratory, for problems that, in Spooner, people call "plumbing problems," but in my educated life people describe as gynecological. I'd like to avoid saying which problems because I was raised not to talk about gynecology, or gall bladders, or livers. "Organ recital," my mother once said about a conversation with a neighbor she'd found indecorous.

My previous surgery had been incomplete because, surprised at the extent of the problem, the doctor ran out of time. Then I got a post-op infection. Was I nervous about my upcoming surgery? No. Between my previous, botched surgery and my upcoming surgery, I'd worked through my post-traumatic-botched-surgery panic by wigging out over a small dental procedure. I didn't want it, I'd said, stubborn. I needed it, people had said, soothing. It's an easy procedure, the oral surgeon had assured me. Right, I'd thought. After the botched, gynecological surgery, I'd battled to stay alive because, answering my phone calls, the heedless surgeon had told me he was sure I didn't have an infection. The oral surgeon had noticed I was scared and promised to be careful.

The oral surgery turned out fine. After it, on a December day, I'd turned fully conscious in Gary's truck as snowflakes fell—rare in Texas—and I saw him in a plate-glass window in a jewelry store, picking up a sized engagement ring, my Christmas present, it turned out, and he'd thought that, drugged, I'd sleep through his errand. The young gynecologist doing my new surgery to repair my old, bad surgery was careful, like the oral surgeon. She'd ordered scans, tests. Gary was busy at work and the kids still in school.

I was thinking about the conference. I was thinking that basil I'd planted was bushy and tender, and I'd make pesto. My phone rang. It was my new doctor calling to move the date of the surgery to August. "Why?" I'd planned for time to recover before teaching again, commuting, the long days—though, if I consider the trade-off between a short commute as a single mother and a long commute as a mother married to a good co-parent, I'm better off. Still, I missed my house in the woods. Everyone plays roles, but maybe more if you move often, advance through social circles, mate and marry a lot. As I'd tried to be what people expected, my self I knew best, my self without veneers, was solo.

My doctor said, "I need an oncologist. This is when he's available."

She'd asked a general surgeon to assist too, three surgeons in all. A long, more intricate surgery, she said. She didn't know for sure that I had cancer because, due to scarring, she couldn't get a tissue sample. But I had three out of three symptoms of uterine cancer. Slow-growing, responsive to treatment, she added. She had to take everything and still fix problems from the previous, botched surgery. She said, "I don't do odds. But if I did, given your history, I'd say your odds of being cancer free are sixty-forty."

This was better than forty-sixty or fifty-fifty, Gary said, when I told him. Better than a successful biopsy that came back positive. I knew, and still know, that everyone who's had worse news than a sixty-forty guess in her favor and nine weeks to find out for sure has had a harder life than me. Gary knew I'd be fine, he said. He'd take care of me always. I was youngish, and even bad news, he said, wouldn't be terrible news. And soon enough we'd face more health issues before, in the end, we'd face more, more, and more.

I didn't find this comforting.

We decided, together, to wait until after the surgery, days after, when pathology results would be back, and we'd tell the children it had been more than routine only if the results were positive. To this day,

Gary insists that he was confident. I followed suit. I read for the conference, book-length manuscripts. I remember the manuscripts, but I don't remember the conference at all, except for leading workshop with willed intensity that, according to the postconference evaluations, students construed as a manic joy of teaching.

After the conference, I had another test, this one involving dye and a balloon. On the way home, I picked up prescriptions, and I lost my keys in a small pharmacy—no big aisles of detergents, makeup, hair brushes, just medicine and sick people—and I retraced my steps, emptied my purse, retraced my steps. A very old man shuffled over. He said, "Have you checked your car, the ignition? They're probably there. Then go home and rest."

When I walked into a room, worry flitted across Gary's face before he put on a hearty manner—to me, indistinguishable from the coded message that I lacked courage, or that he didn't like this agitated version of me. Agitated how? The "responsive to treatment" part of the doctor's call had taken days to register. At first I thought I had to stand weeks of trying not to think about my 60 percent chance not to die, before I understood I had a 60 percent chance not to require chemotherapy, which would be better. And 60 percent, not 50, 40, or worse. Meanwhile, I discovered that I wasn't concerned about life, mine. I'd been my daughter's only parent for her first ten years. She was in middle school. I hadn't lost my mother, available by phone, until I was forty. And I'd had her to see, to spend time with, to touch, until I was in college; I wanted to be that for Marie.

I decided to find a therapist. The therapist said, "Of course, you feel worried, facing mortality." Not a fresh perspective, I thought, as I drove past the city cemetery. Across from it is a business called Beall Memorial Art. In front, a life-sized statue of a man tees off. I was at a red light, staring at the golfing graveyard marker, when the radio started to play a torch song with an emotive vocal dip. Thanatos trumps eros, I thought, alone in heavy traffic. Why did I find a song about lost love cathartic? The vocal dip, the appoggiatura, did its work. Stored memories released. Or darkness encroached. I wanted to get on a highway and go. I'd stop in a bar, get drunk, have a fling, first the distraction of that, then the hangover and hard work of getting to know a stranger.

Not really. Not anymore. Yet I'd cut loose this way for a month or so after high school. For a few years after James Stillman but before I married. After my first divorce, my second. Before I was a mother. Getting acquainted, then the disentangling and back to responsibility—by then, any problem I'd had before the fling was old news. But that life had been shifty, temporary. The light turned green. This life was better. I drove back to it.

AUTHORIZED PERSONNEL ONLY. The doors to the pre-op room opened. Gary's voice was too calm, I thought. He thinks I'm unhinged, like Zea. He's naturally laconic, and his profession has weeded out the extraneous. He says "I love you" when you'd expect: after I say it, or while saying goodbye. "I love you," he said. The anesthesiologist had arrived.

The mask covered my mouth as I stayed calm, pretending I was an adolescent at the lake's edge, waves lapping. No, earlier, a far-off memory, fainter and fainter, like a Xerox of a Xerox: a memory of memory. I lay on a blanket. Above me, trees flex and billow. Their emerald leaves tremble. I've not been a member of the human race for long. An old lady sits nearby. "Gutta," she says. She's gone around the bend, as I've just overheard, maybe during the car ride here. Other women surge inside to see handiwork, leaving me on my blanket and this great-grandmother in her chair. My sister goes inside too. My brother isn't born yet, just a twinkling volition in the life before this, a fist-sized fetus in my mother's belly covered by a new maternity blouse she'd have sewn herself. Stranded with my great-grandmother who calls out, "Don't leave me," I understand our situations—if not the two of us—are dead ringers. Left to fend for ourselves, we're doomed.

"There." A post-op nurse changed my IV and wheeled me to my room.

I went home. When the phone call about the pathology report came, negative, I was strangely blasé, sedated. I longed irrationally for busy work, for a sewing basket I no longer owned. I didn't have glossy and colorful skeins, stamped pillowslips, my hoop, my tiny jeweled scissors from Garnett's store. I thought, I'm going to be a cranky old lady. Marie thinks so. I cuss when I'm multitasking: cooking while grading; vacuuming while stopping to add a line to a paragraph. "All this cussing will spill out when you're old and in a hospital, and I'm going to have to explain to the nurses that you're otherwise polite."

I didn't feel polite, even with familiar pictures on the bedroom wall, lace curtains Gary had grudgingly said he liked here, in private. I trudged to the living room, admiring a chair I bought in Utah, a table from North Carolina, a cabinet from Gary's parents' house. I remembered Gary saying this house would be our last with stairs. "We can still have front steps," I yelled. "I'm not ready for a goddamn wheelchair ramp yet." But he wasn't home. Who was? My friend from Vermont, my long-distance friend Gary had sent for because she has an almost paranormal ability to understand people's feelings, and she's a medical reporter. She eased me to the couch, saying, "He's out filling one of your prescriptions."

She kept an eye on me while finishing her daily blog for *FiercePharma*, then doing her exercises, Brute Yoga. I listened to the clicking of her laptop keyboard. Then I watched her curve into C-shapes, S-shapes. "Gary never believed I might really be sick," I said. She said, "He's been terrified. He doesn't know how to help in the ways you want," she added, her smiling face upside-down between her legs, "and that's why I'm here."

Gary came in with my prescription, also two bouquets of flowers, one for the bedroom, he said, the other for the living room, because my friend from Vermont, the empath who's a medical reporter, had told him I'd want to move around, a change of scenery.

The doctor had said to take two pain pills, one too many I realized during a phone call with my sister who'd called to say she loved me, her instilled kindness. We agreed that the geographical distance is hard. Yet I've never been able to convince my family that it wasn't mere choice to live far from Spooner, that my career had required most moves. But Gary's family proved to me that shared geography keeps a shared language intact, a language of hearth, home, meals, chores, family lore. The new language of work had connected me to new people, a network, and I'd moved up, around, sideways, and forward.

I felt dizzy—and maybe it was just me, confused, defensive—as the phone conversation drifted to the idea that I hadn't tried to stay close, and I said I had, visiting, calling. I'd felt like a ventriloquist, projecting this voice here, that voice there. "All of me tried hard," I said, standing, woozy, and I must have sounded shrill, because Gary was taking the phone away, saying into it that I was sick, his hearty manner turned up high, helpful.

My dad called Gary, asking how I was, then shouting so loud I heard it: "Praise the Lord." My dad didn't have this exclamatory tic when I was little. Lutherans sing it, but he got in the habit of saying it at his all-school reunion, he told Gary, due to an old classmate, Gloria, renamed GloryB now. "Sounds like a fun reunion," Gary said, still watching baseball. When Gary hung up, I said, "Thank you." He smiled at me. "No problem."

My friend went back to Vermont. Fraiser came home from his mother's.

Marie understood I'd had a surgery, and then forgot. Gary had brought her to my hospital room, straight from her summer internship teaching tumbling, and she'd looked at the tubes, the IVs, and got mad. "Why didn't you say?" But at home I couldn't sit all the way up for weeks because an interior seam tore and had to be redone; she got used to me reclined. Gary drove me around with the passenger seat flat. Treetops, light poles, buildings flew by. He helped me out of the car, holding my purse. He'd been right, if too far in the future, losing sight of now, when he'd said that this would be a rehearsal for the end.

One day, I lay on the couch thinking that life is a race, a skirmish. You try to be like everyone, but not exactly, because you're supposed to rise above the fray, the fray a cluster of kinship, and strangers too, some of whom become kin, akin, and then the fray unravels.

School began again—for Fraiser, for Marie. I was on medical leave. Fraiser came in and started his homework. Gary was unpacking groceries. Marie arrived full of news about algebra, other students, teachers, history, a dance, boys, and she was standing a few steps up the staircase, and I was lying down, and I thought it was good she didn't know how confusing it will be to secure her place in the world. None of us knows because being young is oblivion, nirvana, that hard-wired impulse to suppress some if not most of our parents' warnings and directives. But I wouldn't change the unsystematic approach by which I got to here, I thought. Here is right. Marie said, "You're not sad or anything?"

"Not sad," I said.

She said, "Good. Because I have to tell you. I need new shoes again." I must have looked exasperated. She said, "I can't help it. The ones I just got—they're already all wrong."

I break with tradition then, using weddings as a means to my end, not The End, ending instead with two funerals and a complicated hysterectomy. But I'm not morbid. I don't think about my body—guts, bones, protoplasm, a container of fear and desire—as something to monitor for signs of decline, not yet. One Sunday I was thinking how well fed I'd felt after I'd returned from brunch with new friends, all of us married, three of us mothers, all of us writers, and the conversation had flown between recipes, books, work, shopping, and then I hurried home, where I was making a pot roast while preparing to teach the next day. I was still dressed up, including lipstick, red: mimicking the state of receptivity in female mammals known as estrus, from the Latin word for *frenzy, gadfly, sting*.

Marie was asking about a sleepover. Fraiser wanted to know when we'd eat. I was completing two tasks at once while answering questions, which makes me impatient, and then Gary walked in my study and asked for help finding the car title for the car I'd driven until lately, a car Fraiser would drive now. I said, "Find the one file folder with my handwriting on it." I'd marked a file BIRTH, MARRIAGES, DIVORCES but kept all my legal documents in it. Gary, on the other hand, has chronologically arranged years of careful record-keeping: policies, statements, taxes. He organizes and reorganizes closets, cupboards, the refrigerator. He's devised a system in the laundry room for our recyclable trash.

When I'd moved to Austin, I'd separated essential documents from the merely memorable, emptying a stack of drawers that serves as a center column for a table, drop leaf on both sides, that had been my mother's sewing table. She'd slid out leaves for a surface on which to cut fabric, and she'd stowed thread, patterns, pins—"notions"—in its drawers. When my parents divvied up furniture, I'd taken this table with its shape-changing properties (both leaves up, both down, left or right up or down) for various places I'd live. I'd filled the drawers with papers, receipts, letters, diplomas. When I moved, I'd kept vital records—proof that I existed, that I'd married and divorced, proof that Marie existed—in one folder. When I packed, I slid it in a box. When I unpacked, I put it in Gary's filing cabinet. The sewing table was in Fraiser's room now, one leaf up, a desk.

When Gary and I had applied for our license to marry, I'd opened this BIRTH, MARRIAGES, DIVORCES file folder and quickly found my birth certificate and second divorce decree. Afterward, I put them back inside. Our own Rites of Marriage certificate was so beautiful, with scrolling letters and a gold seal—the same design the courthouse had used for a hundred years, the woman had said when Gary and I picked it up—that I'd put it in an antique frame and hung it on the wall. So the last time I'd looked inside the BIRTH, MARRIAGES, DIVORCES file slowly was years earlier, when my second ex-husband, Chet, had called because he was marrying a woman who wasn't a U.S. citizen, and she couldn't get immigration status until he proved he was divorced. He didn't know when or where I'd filed. Did I have a case number? His mother had said: "Find Debra. She was good with paperwork."

In this same phone call, Chet had said his mother and her imperious, unpleasant husband, my father-in-law #2, had divorced. Chet recounted a story so odd it sounded untrue. Chet's mother told him she'd found her husband in his office, having sex with a man while she'd been next door, typing. Chet sounded baffled, uncertain, yet he was sure of the next part. The crazy grandma had died and left everyone, including Chet, land. The crazy grandma left her money to Chet's mother, a considerable sum that should have been used to finish converting the hunting camp to a house, but Chet's stepfather had craved world travel and spent the money. My mother-in-law #2 was old, twice-divorced, and broke.

A sad story unconnected to me, I thought.

Because now I was married to Gary, who was standing in my study, saying, "I know you can picture this file folder, but I can't. Please stop working and help me find it."

I opened the file cabinet, found the file folder, located the car title, and gave it to Gary. Then I noticed a sheaf of legal-sized papers, like a deed or decree, folded, typed, not word-processed. I unfolded it. "The Family History of the Grosskopfs and the Schades in Fayette County." First, at the top, a diagram. "Great-Grandfather, Patrilineal + Great-Grandmother, Patrilineal, Grosskopf" and "Great-Grandfather, Matrilineal + Great-Grandmother, Matrilineal, Schade." Then the pyramid of descendants. Then the narrative. Fayette County is Gary's family's county. I said, "This must have fallen out of one of your files and got stuck in mine. Or it belongs with your parents' papers."

Gary glanced at it. "I've never heard of these people."

I said, "I'm not from Fayette County. It can't be mine." I checked the pot roast and went back to my study. When I came out, I heard Marie in her room listening to hip-hop, slightly louder than Fraiser listening to alt-rock. I went to the TV room, next to the laundry room. Gary was doing laundry. The dryer hummed companionably, and Gary had on the TV, an ESPN show about baseball managers preparing for spring, old players, new players, prospects. He was still reading "The Family History of the Grosskopfs and the Schades in Fayette County." He said, "What a vile cross-section of humanity." Then, "It amazes me that anyone would record this." Then, "Debra, these are your old in-laws."

The name Grosskopf suddenly clicked. Chet's crazy grandma's last name, his mother's maiden name. Schade would be the crazy grandma's maiden name. I don't have a bad memory, but it's idiosyncratic. I recalled standing in the dining room in Salt Lake City, talking on Chet's new phone, high-tech at the time, and his mother saying she'd researched her family, written up the results, and she'd mail us a copy. I'd never read "The Family History of the Grosskopfs and the Schades in Fayette County," but I'm good with paperwork, as she'd said, so I'd put Chet's family history in my mother's sewing table and moved to North Carolina, then Texas. Who knows when I'd stuffed it into my BIRTH, MARRIAGES, DIVORCES file? "The Family History of the Gross-kopfs and the Schades in Fayette County" had rubbed against my vital papers, my daughter's, and now Gary's.

I went back to my study and used the Internet to search Chet's mother's name. She was working for Chet on a plot of land down that driveway I'd passed coming home from Gary's Aunt Alvina's funeral. Chet owned a vineyard now, apparently. Reading the vineyard website, the "About Us" section, I recognized Chet's pet phrases: "deal-flow," "as per client specifications." He employed ninety people. Annual profits over a million dollars. I exited the website. Then I felt sure I'd misread. I retyped the name of the vineyard, and a social-media-for-companies website came up. Someone had posted a different descrip-tion. The vineyard employed three people: Chet, his wife, his mother. The profits were a fraction of a fraction of a million. Then I felt tawdry, cyberstalking, and quit.

I went back to the TV room, where "The Family History of the Grosskopfs and the Schades in Fayette County" lay on the table, and I thought how family trees begin with two people who marry, inaugurat-ing a lineage. When we mate, we end up with who we end up because of location and practical math—one nearby single and one nearby single become a pair—also hormonal surges that are part of love but aren't love. "I fell in lust all over again," an old friend from graduate school, living in Ohio, once said by phone. The reasons for this or that mar-riage, for this and that begetting, for anybody's family history—which brings tears to the eye, creates genealogy junkies, and compels people to join the Daughters of the American Revolution—is happenstance.

Yet we turn out like our ancestors, biologically and biographically pro-grammed, imitators by nature and by nurture.

I'd been connected to two ex-husbands, two family lines that might have stayed connected to mine. I'd pledged myself to a few other men, other potential family lines that might, in time, have attached to me. I sometimes wake in the middle of the night next to Gary, light peeping around the edge of curtains, and I see the outlines of our room, fur-nishings, bits and pieces, some new, most old, and I've been dream-ing about one of my ex-husbands or ex-boyfriends, a long-gone, dis-placed former someone, and in the dream the man is the age he was when I knew him, but I'm who I am now, and I don't know what to say to him, younger, so green, ready to master life with skills he has avail-able.

As I sat in the TV room that Sunday, pot roast bubbling on the stove in the kitchen, the sun outside the windows starting to sink, I thought about these dreams, exes as mental excess, my end credits rolling. I met Rodney V. Meadow at a fair. In dreams, he leans in, a crooked smile. He died of a heart attack, survived by his mother and sister. My father had called to tell me. The obituary mentioned a dog as survivor too, my dad had said, puzzled. It was the second time someone called to tell me someone I'd known, *known*, was dead, that a body I'd held had transmuted to another state. James Stillman is dead too, but in dreams he frowns, putting cocaine on a mirror, or restringing an elec-tric guitar.

In one dream, I sit with him in the dining room, and he's in his twenties, still hoping we'll get back together. He's staying with us be-cause he wants to return to college and needs help with the applica-tion, his statement of purpose. I'm line-editing while advising him to start with a lofty sense of resolve and end with practical facts. In the dream, Gary summons me to speak privately in another room. Gary says, "He's had a hard life and needs a hand up. I don't begrudge that. So help him with this application. But he can't stay here, not with the kids—it's too disruptive." I nod, because our kids, closer to James's age, matter most. In the dining room I tell James that when we finish this statement of purpose he has to go. Next he's gone, forever unfinished.

In this era of late marriages to someone who has a past, this era of second and third marriages, a new branch of psychotherapy has sprung up, devoted to mourning one's previous mates. Ambiguous Grief. And people will hurry to tell you about a death because they feel swollen with the news, sideswiped, since death will come for them too, and not knowing what to do with this death relief, death sympathy, death freight—"death is weird," a woman said at the literary festival the night my mother-in-law died—they'll call.

Joe, half-orphaned, wanted in Indiana, lives in Indiana, retired. He must have paid his child support, or cut a deal, or enough time had passed, I'd thought, when he wrote to me at my university email address—or he'd dictated to his sister, who owned a computer, and her name is Jackie_and_Jim19834—and Joe was friendly, too friendly, via his sister, amanuensis. Like it was yesteryear. I wished him well; I said I was married. He wrote once more to say his sister wouldn't write for him again after she found out I was married.

My ex-husband #1 has stayed nameless in this book, except for this: I kept his name. I never took Chet's, saying I'd already earned one graduate degree with the name *Monroe*. But in fact I like the way it sounds. In Utah and North Carolina, people who didn't know I hadn't taken Chet's name called me Mrs. Crosswater. And it was difficult to explain to even feminists that I'd kept my name, since it wasn't mine, just a former husband's, and no I didn't still want him, just his euphonious name. I'd loved his family too. During a trip to Wisconsin, a trip at Christmastime, when clans gather, one of the brothers of my ex-husband #1 arranged to meet me for dinner in Eau Claire. My former brother-in-law had said, "Mom says hi. Dad says hi. Polly says hi. Jon says hi. Luke says hi. Jenny says hi." Everyone said hi except my ex-husband #1, who might have, my former brother-in-law explained, except my ex-husband #1's new wife would have gotten mad.

In terms of the "What I Want to Be When I Grow Up" checklist, my options—Mother, Nurse, Teacher, Secretary, Stewardess, and Other—

I could have been Rodney's casserole-making wife, ex-wife or widow by now. Or forever Queenie. Or a groupie turned aging band wife. Or a girlfriend helping out on movie sets and spending spare time in an adobe dance hall. Or a lady professor waiting for poetic letters. Reader, it's safe to say that I grew up to be Other, and this was my evolution, not a plan.

One day when both kids had been gone for a week, Fraiser on a vacation with his mother, Marie at camp, I'd told Gary—shouted it, because I was in the tub, floating, inspecting marks on my stomach from incisions, operations that turned out fine—that I'd had a great week, that I loved our kids, our life. Gary stood in the door and said, "I had a great week too." He added that he hoped we had plenty of time left, that one of us will outlive the other, of course, and then he started in with how we hope for an active life, a swift death, and no painful lingering. I'd said, "Please shut up. It's important to have a few conversations about end-of-life scenarios. But not over and over." He'd laughed, agreeing.

Right now, on a winter afternoon, he was watching the Major League Baseball General Managers Meeting coverage in earnest. I picked up "The Family History of the Grosskopfs and the Schades in Fayette County" and read. So-and-so found poisoned in the barn, no one arrested, but people thought it was the wife, who later turned up in a bar in Louisiana. So-and-so known for setting up the region's first school, from which he embezzled, found floating in a cattle tank. So-and-so raped, or possibly not, because she had a history of lying, but her brothers hunted down the man she'd accused and lit him on fire.

I'd hurtled through someone else's history. Near miss.

Almost mine.

These people had been dead for years. And yet, I thought, the descendants had descended.

I threw the family history onto the table. "It's gruesome."

Gary looked up. "We all have forerunners who were black sheep."

Yet not so many, not so menacing, I thought. The colorful figure in my family is a grandfather who'd been with a vamp and gambled. My wandering grandmother had schizophrenia. They seem no more unusual than you or me, or someone you or I know who's had affairs or a mental health diagnosis. Yet the fog of history, the unfamiliarity of the vistas—a fur coat and a roadster, a sod house and a corncrib— make them exotic. My ancestors may have been unevenly educated, badly matched, stuck in the centrifugal whirl of centuries of tradition: women who wait on men. And there were hard stories in Gary's family too. But no one had murdered or embezzled or perjured or lit someone on fire.

"The Family History of the Grosskopfs and Schades in Fayette County" was scary in reverse, a road I'd started to take, then turned back. I said, "I'm going to throw this in the trash," realizing that even if I got rid of the paper record I wasn't getting rid of the history, none of it, none of my irregular past, evidence I'd had a vagrant heart but a sense of direction too, an inclination toward the dark side, but the alchemy of luck had converted it to light. Gary, still watching TV, said, "You mean the recycling."

ACKNOWLEDGMENTS

I dedicate this book to the memory of Kit Ward, who first encouraged me to write it. My best thanks to David Meischen, my hard-core, astute, page-by-page reader. Thank you as well to David McGlynn, Donna Johnson, John Dufresne, Shen Christenson, Scott Blackwood, and John Griswold. Thank you to Kathryn Lang, who taught me so much ("Debra, this is your life!"). Thank you to Summer Wood and Bob Shacochis for help in the dog days of summer. I thank editors of the following publications in which excerpts and sometimes bits or traces of this book were previously published: *Longreads.com*; the *American Scholar*; the *Morning News*; the *Southern Review*; the *Florida Review*; *RACAonline*; *Inside Higher Ed*. Thank you to my absolutely wonderful agent, Jane Gelfman, and to Lisa Bayer and Elizabeth Crowley.

To Gary, Fraiser, and Marie: XXOO.

AUTHOR'S NOTE

For the sake of other people's privacy, I've changed some names, as I've clearly indicated in the book. Sometimes, when a name was too ideal, too allegorical, I just couldn't, as I've also indicated. For the same reason—because I'm telling my story, not anyone else's—I've changed some identifying details about some secondary characters.